12/10

Merry
Christma...

Dad/Gramp

Love, Michele + Angela

IRISH TRIVIA

ON TAP

IRISH TRIVIA
ON TAP

600 questions to measure your IQ

(irish quotient)

JENNIFER GRACE

FALL RIVER PRESS

Book design by Michele Trombley

Fall River Press
122 Fifth Avenue
New York, NY 10011

ISBN: 978-1-4351-1588-0

Printed and bound in the United States of America

3   5   7   9   10   8   6   4   2

acknowledgments

Special thanks to my husband, Peter, for being my everything, and to his boys, Scott, Taylor, Campbell, and PJ for being such great additions to my life. To my family, whose support, love, and undeniable sense of humor have carried me through life.

To my editors, Heather Rodino and Ruth O'Brien, you have made this process a joy. And, of course, to my publisher, Bruce Lubin, a dear friend and colleague; you're a gem.

To Finn Hayden, who's living proof that there's a little Irish in everyone, and to his mom and my co-writer, Signe, whose writing skills and friendship I couldn't live with without.

contents

introduction

Life's too short not to be Irish!
—Irish saying

Ireland may be a relatively tiny island, but it has one of the world's finest cultural heritages. What other culture celebrates the luck of the leprechaun, takes pride in one's readiness to fight, and allows you to demand a kiss? *Irish Trivia on Tap* gives you more than 600 questions that will provide you with loads of *craic* (fun) while testing your IQ (Irish Quotient). Featuring tons of trivia, whimsical tidbits of information, and charming anecdotes that cover everything from sinners and saints to Guinness, this book brings the Emerald Isle to vibrant life. From the influence of the Vikings to U2's blockbuster hits and from Daniel O'Connell to Michael Collins, *Irish Trivia on Tap* sheds light on the timeless spirit of the Irish people, leaving no stone—Blarney or otherwise—unturned. So get "craic-ing" and test the level of "Irish" in your blood, whether it's a pint or only a drop. After all, whatever one's nationality, everybody has a wee bit of Irish in them.

chapter 1

Writers, Musicians, and Actors, Oh, My!
Arts and Entertainment

Ireland is where strange tales begin and happy endings are possible.
—Charles Haughey

1. What did Cedric Gibbons design?

    a. The Oscar statuette

    b. The Celtic cross

    c. The bodhran

    d. The Guinness logo

2. Who wrote *Angela's Ashes*?

    a. Jonathan Swift

    b. Maeve Binchy

    c. Frank McCourt

    d. Stephen Roche

3. William Butler Yeats was awarded the Nobel Prize in Literature in what year?

    a. 1943

    b. 1923

    c. 1933

    d. 1953

4. Which Irish writer left Ireland for London after the banning of the book *The Dark*?

    a. Edmund Burke

    b. Thomas Gray

    c. Maud Gonne

    d. John McGahern

5. Who is Neil Jordan?

    a. A famous hurler

    b. The Academy Award–winning screenplay writer of *The Crying Game*

    c. The writer of *Against All Odds*

    d. The only Irish man to win the Tour de France

6. Which of these films does not feature Irish culture?

    a. *Angela's Ashes*

    b. *The Butcher Boy*

    c. *Sling Blade*

    d. *Waking Ned Divine*

7. Before joining U2, drummer Larry Mullen Jr. was a member of which band?

    a. Artane Boys' Band

    b. A Flock of Seagulls

    c. Thin Lizzy

    d. The Gallagher Group

8. In 1910, English lawyer Frederick Weatherly wrote what famous Irish song?

    a. "Dirty Old Town"

    b. "Green Fields of France"

    c. "Danny Boy"

    d. "A Nation Once Again"

9. *Riverdance* high-kicked its way into the spotlight during what 1994 contest?

    a. Eurovision Song Contest

    b. Ride On Contest

    c. The Gaelic League Contest

    d. The Dubliners Contest

10. Who is Michael Flatley?

    a. Producer and director of *Lord of the Dance*

    b. A singer and harpist

    c. A boxer

    d. A sound engineer

11. Which band got their big break in 1978 upon winning a talent contest sponsored by Guinness?

    a. Stiff Little Fingers

    b. Thin Lizzy

    c. U2

    d. Horslips

12. What is the Bord Scannán na hÉireann?

    a. The Restaurant Review Board

    b. The Irish Film Board

    c. The Arts Review Board

    d. The Board of Journalism

13. Academy Award–winner and Irishman Daniel Day-Lewis did not appear in which of the following films?

    a. *My Left Foot*

    b. *There Will Be Blood*

    c. *I Went Down*

    d. *Gangs of New York*

14. **Which Shakespearean actor earned the respect of the Irish for turning down knighthood?**

    a. Kenneth Branagh
    b. Peter O'Toole
    c. Daniel Day-Lewis
    d. Colm Meaney

15. **Name the county town in Mayo that was featured in John Ford's *The Quiet Man*.**

    a. Castlebar
    b. Kilkenny
    c. Enniskillen
    d. Cong

16. **To whom did William Butler Yeats dedicate much of his love poetry?**

    a. Maud Gonne
    b. Lady Gregory
    c. Cathleen Houlihan
    d. Georgie Hyde Lees

17. **What language was the *Book of Kells* written in?**

    a. Gaelic
    b. French
    c. Latin
    d. Old Irish

18. **Give the last word in the title of the following book by Roddy Doyle: *The Woman Who Walked Into* _____.**

    a. Mirrors
    b. Windows
    c. Water
    d. Doors

19. After which Dublin road does Maeve Binchy name her 1999 novel?

a. Tara
b. Auburn
c. Friar
d. Down

the literary life

Match the author with his or her work.

A. James Joyce
B. John McGahern
C. Flann O'Brien
D. John Banville
E. Bram Stoker
F. Edna O'Brien
G. Elizabeth Bowen
H. Jennifer Johnston
I. Brian Moore
J. James Plunkett
K. Maria Edgeworth
L. Kate O'Brien
M. Patrick Kavanagh
N. Samuel Beckett
O. Laurence Sterne

1. *The Land of Spices*
2. *Ulysses*
3. *Judith Hearne*
4. *The Country Girls*
5. *The Last September*
6. *The Book of Evidence*
7. *Strumpet City*
8. *Castle Rackrent*
9. *At Swim-Two-Birds*
10. *Tarry Flynn*
11. *The Life and Opinions of Tristram Shandy, Gentleman*
12. *Murphy*
13. *How Many Miles to Babylon?*
14. *Dracula*
15. *Amongst Women*

Answers: A, 2; B, 15; C, 9; D, 6; E, 14; F, 4; G, 5; H, 13; I, 3; J, 7; K, 8; L, 1; M, 10; N, 12; O, 11

20. Which author won the Irish Press Hennessy Award for the short story "The Call" while working as a teacher at Kingsbury Day Special School?

    a. Elizabeth Bowen
    b. Molly Keane
    c. Aidan Higgins
    d. Patrick McCabe

21. Which of the following musicians is *not* of Irish ancestry?

    a. Enya
    b. Mary Black
    c. Nick Cave
    d. Elvis Costello

22. What is the real name of U2's lead singer, Bono?

    a. Larry Mullen Jr.
    b. Paul Hewson
    c. Patrick Clayton
    d. Adam Evans

23. Who wrote the lyrics "You can't stop us on the road to freedom / You can't stop us 'cause our eyes can see…"?

    a. Van Morrison
    b. Rory Gallagher
    c. Phil Lynott
    d. Christy Moore

24. Which band had a huge hit with the Christmas carol "Fairytale of New York"?

    a. The Boomtown Rats

    b. The Undertones

    c. The Pogues

    d. The Chieftains

25. Who went to the top of the *Billboard* charts with a song penned by Prince?

    a. Sinéad O'Connor

    b. Noel Hill

    c. Shane MacGowan

    d. Luka Bloom

26. In Jim Sheridan's *My Left Foot*, Daniel Day-Lewis portrays the life of this Irish author, painter, and poet:

    a. Christy Brown

    b. Robert Collis

    c. Cecil Day-Lewis

    d. Frank O'Connor

27. The original title of *My Left Foot* is also the name of this popular song by The Pogues:

    a. "Boy from the County Hell"

    b. "Dirty Old Town"

    c. "If I Should Fall from Grace with God"

    d. "Down All the Days"

28. Considered the "second Olivier," this actor made his first appearance on the London stage in Jane Arden's *The Party*:

    a. Aidan Quinn
    b. Albert Finney
    c. Gabriel Byrne
    d. Cillian Murphy

29. Which actor first gained popularity with the television show *Remington Steele*?

    a. Pierce Brosnan
    b. Liam Neeson
    c. Jonathan Rhys Meyers
    d. Stephen Rea

30. This Irish journalist turned a collection of columns into a best-selling memoir:

    a. Edna O'Brien
    b. Ann Moore
    c. Marian Keyes
    d. Nuala O'Faolain

31. Who wrote, "I could not write the words Mr. Joyce uses: my prudish hands would refuse to form the letters"?

    a. Ernest Hemingway
    b. Virginia Woolf
    c. George Bernard Shaw
    d. Dave Eggers

32. How many Irishmen have won the Nobel Prize in Literature?

    a. Five

    b. Three

    c. None

    d. Two

33. What novel begins, "Stately plump Buck Mulligan came from the stairhead, bearing a bowl of lather on which a mirror and a razor lay crossed"?

    a. *The Nation*

    b. *Mulligan*

    c. *Ulysses*

    d. *Finnegans Wake*

34. Which famous Irish actress died in 1986?

    a. Grace Kelly

    b. Maureen O'Hara

    c. Siobhán McKenna

    d. Maud Gonne

35. Which famous Irish writer of short stories was born in Cork in 1903?

    a. Mary Lavin

    b. Frank O'Connor

    c. James Joyce

    d. Sherwood Anderson

36. What is Ireland's most popular national theater?

    a. The Abbey Theatre

    b. The Olympia Theatre

    c. The Gate Theatre

    d. The Gaiety Theatre

37. What Dublin theater is a converted nineteenth-century train terminal?

    a. The Abbey Theatre

    b. The Theatre Royal

    c. The O_2 (originally the Point Theatre)

    d. The Gate Theatre

38. Who wrote the novel *Trinity*?

    a. Leon Uris

    b. William Kennedy

    c. Paul Henry

    d. Graham Reid

39. What John Ford film set in Dublin received an Academy Awards nomination for Best Picture?

    a. *The Searchers*

    b. *How Green Was My Valley*

    c. *The Informer*

    d. *The Whole Town's Talking*

40. In the film *The Irish in Us*, which actors play the roles of brothers Danny O'Hara and Pat O'Hara?

    a. Allen Jenkins and Frank McHugh

    b. James Stewart and J. Farrell MacDonald

    c. Harvey Parry and Thomas E. Jackson

    d. James Cagney and Pat O'Brien

41. Who wrote "An Elegy on the Death of a Mad Dog," which ends with the words "The man recovered of the bite / The dog it was that died"?

    a. Oliver Goldsmith

    b. Thomas Moore

    c. Jonathan Swift

    d. Tommy Makem

42. Put the following films in chronological order, from earliest to latest: *Irish Eyes Are Smiling, My Wild Irish Rose, Untamed.*

    a. *Untamed* (1935), *Irish Eyes Are Smiling* (1944), *My Wild Irish Rose* (1957)

    b. *Irish Eyes Are Smiling* (1944), *Untamed* (1946), *My Wild Irish Rose* (1947)

    c. *Irish Eyes Are Smiling* (1944), *My Wild Irish Rose* (1947), *Untamed* (1955)

    d. *My Wild Irish Rose* (1947), *Irish Eyes Are Smiling* (1950), *Untamed* (1955)

43. Which film tells the story of an Irish woman who becomes a Nazi spy because of her hatred for England?

    a. *I See a Dark Stranger*

    b. *Odd Man Out*

    c. *The Luck of the Irish*

    d. *Shake Hands with the Devil*

JAMES JOYCE (1882–1941)

A statue of James Joyce created by Marjorie Fitzgibbon in 1990 stands on the corner of North Earl and O'Connell streets in Dublin, where it commemorates the life and work of one of Ireland's most famous authors. Joyce catalogued the lives of the city's residents in *Dubliners* and once claimed that if Dublin were ever destroyed, it could be reconstructed through the pages of his 1922 masterpiece *Ulysses*. Despite the love reserved for the author today, the Irish originally branded *Ulysses* pornographic and banned it. The ban was not lifted until the 1960s.

44. John Ford's *The Rising of the Moon* is based on short stories by which authors?

    a. James Joyce, William Butler Yeats, Oscar Wilde

    b. Lady Gregory, Michael McHugh, Frank O'Connor

    c. John McCormack, Frank Patterson, Josef Locke

    d. Samuel Beckett, Edna O'Brien, John McGahern

45. Fluther Good is a character from what Sean O'Casey play?

    a. *The Plough and the Stars*

    b. *The Shadow of a Gunman*

    c. *Juno and the Paycock*

    d. *The Playboy of the Western World*

46. Who directed the 1987 movie _The Dead_, which was based on James Joyce's story of the same name?

    a. Merchant Ivory

    b. John Ford

    c. John Huston

    d. Francis Ford Coppola

47. What Irish poem concerns the dream of a man who finds himself in a court ruled by women and inquiring into the state of Irish men?

    a. _The Red Bull_

    b. _The Death of Cúchulainn_

    c. _The Midnight Court_

    d. _Castle Rackrent_

48. Who stars in Francis Ford Coppola's _Finian's Rainbow_?

    a. Fred Astaire

    b. Gene Kelly

    c. Stanley Donen

    d. James Mason

49. Who wrote Ireland's biggest selling single of all time, "I Useta Lover"?

    a. The Saw Doctors

    b. U2

    c. The Cranberries

    d. Van Morrison

50. The band The Boomtown Rats got their name from which of the following?

a. An Irish rugby team
b. A Dublin pub
c. A book by Woody Guthrie
d. Irish slang

51. To whom did Bono refer as "one of the top ten players of all time"?

a. The Edge
b. Rory Gallagher
c. Van Morrison
d. Bob Geldof

52. Which Irish artist performed with The Band in the concert film *The Last Waltz*?

a. Bono
b. Phil Lynott
c. Van Morrison
d. Elvis Costello

53. In what rock opus did Bob Geldof play a prominent role?

a. *Tommy*
b. *Quadrophenia*
c. *The Wall*
d. *Sgt. Pepper's Lonely Hearts Club Band*

54. **Before joining Led Zeppelin, Jimmy Page was a session guitarist on an album by which Irish group?**

    a. Thin Lizzy
    b. Them
    c. The Boomtown Rats
    d. U2

55. **Elvis Costello's great-grandfather was born in County Tyrone, Ireland. Where was Elvis Costello born?**

    a. Ballyshannon, County Donegal
    b. Belfast, Northern Ireland
    c. Dun Laoghaire, County Dublin
    d. Paddington, Greater London

56. **Who wrote the poems "Easter, 1916" and "The Wild Swans at Coole"?**

    a. William Butler Yeats
    b. Seamus Deane
    c. Seamus Heaney
    d. Patrick McCabe

57. **Which play by John Millington Synge caused riots when it first appeared on the stage in Dublin?**

    a. *Riders to the Sea*
    b. *The Playboy of the Western World*
    c. *The Shadow of the Glen*
    d. *The Well of the Saints*

58. Which artist quipped, upon entering U.S. customs, "I have nothing to declare except my genius"?

    a. Patrick McCabe

    b. Jonathan Swift

    c. Oscar Wilde

    d. Seamus Deane

59. Which winner of the Nobel Prize in Literature is also well known for his translation of *Beowulf*?

    a. Seamus Heaney

    b. William Butler Yeats

    c. Samuel Beckett

    d. George Bernard Shaw

60. This novel's first line is the completion of a sentence begun on the last line of the novel.

    a. *Finnegans Wake*

    b. *A Portrait of the Artist as a Young Man*

    c. *Ulysses*

    d. *Gulliver's Travels*

61. Which book was turned into a movie starring Eamonn Owens?

    a. *Roddy Doyle*

    b. *Carna*

    c. *The Butcher Boy*

    d. *Sleeper*

62. By what name was the Irish writer Æ also known?

    a. Arthur Edgar

    b. George Russell

    c. Francis Ledwidge

    d. Samuel Beckett

63. What instrument is James Galway famous for playing?

    a. Harp

    b. Harmonica

    c. Flute

    d. Trombone

64. What is Rosemary Brown's professional name?

    a. Enya

    b. Briquette

    c. Mumba

    d. Dana

65. Who sang "Have I Told You Lately" with Van Morrison?

    a. The Cranberries

    b. The Dubliners

    c. Enya

    d. The Chieftains

66. Who wrote the Irish national anthem?

    a. Peadar Kearney

    b. Brendan Behan

    c. George M. Cohan

    d. William Butler Yeats

67. What did Jonathan Swift's *A Modest Proposal* propose exactly?

a. A solution to Ireland's potato famine
b. The selling of children as food, to solve Ireland's economic problems
c. A system of religious reform
d. Legislative parameters for voting rights

68. Which famous Irish singer was given the title of papal count in 1928?

a. Josef Locke
b. Frank Patterson
c. John McCormack
d. Packie Dolan

69. The song "Do They Know It's Christmas?" was cowritten by Bob Geldof and which other artist?

a. Jimmy MacCarthy
b. Enya
c. John Field
d. Midge Ure

chapter 2

Leprechauns, Banshees, and Spells:
Superstitions and Folklore

*May the saddest day of your future be no worse
than the happiest day of your past.*
—Irish blessing

1. What is a traditional Irish cure for a hangover?

    a. To be buried up to the neck in moist river sand

    b. A hair of the dog

    c. Corned beef and cabbage

    d. A swift kick in the shin

2. What does the traditional superstition "a Saturday flit is a short sit" mean?

    a. If you move to a new house on a Saturday, disaster is sure to follow

    b. If you make plans for a first date on a Saturday, disaster is sure to follow

    c. If you exercise on a Saturday, disaster is sure to follow

    d. If you visit your in-laws on a Saturday, disaster is sure to follow

3. To the Irish, if you give a friend a prayer book, what are you saying?

    a. The friendship is blessed

    b. The friendship is over

    c. The friendship is a gift

    d. The friendship has begun anew

4. What will seeing one magpie supposedly bring you?

    a. Love

    b. Happiness

    c. Money

    d. Sorrow

5. What is seeing five magpies said to bring you?

    a. A spouse

    b. A home

    c. Silver

    d. Fame

6. According to Irish folklore, what are hawthorn sticks?

    a. Powerful wands

    b. Candles

    c. Crystal necklaces

    d. Canes

7. According to legend, what well-known geographical formation did the devil spit out?

    a. The Rock of Cashel

    b. The Valley of Ulster

    c. The Slieve Bloom Mountains

    d. The Saltee Islands

8. Irish superstition holds that if you fall and touch the ground at a cemetery, what will most likely happen by the end of the year?

   a. You'll have a baby
   b. You'll die
   c. You'll get rich
   d. You'll have bad luck

9. When knives lie crossed on the countertop or table, what does this mean?

   a. A male visitor is coming
   b. A female visitor is coming
   c. There's going to be a household argument
   d. You're about to receive money from a stranger

10. Fill in the blanks: A _____ hen, a _____ girl, and a _____ cat are considered very _____.

   a. Fat, little, white, lucky
   b. Skinny, happy, fat, unlucky
   c. Crowing, whistling, black, unlucky
   d. Spotted, skipping, black, unlucky

11. According to Irish folklore, what should one do to remedy disorders of the stomach?

   a. Imbibe a belt of whiskey
   b. Tie a bunch of mint around one's wrist
   c. Hang a horseshoe on the doorpost
   d. Place one's bed in an east-facing direction

12. What is an iron ring worn on the fourth finger said to ward off?

    a. Memory loss

    b. A headache

    c. Fever

    d. Rheumatism

13. What should you put in your friend's coat if you want him to win at cards?

    a. A spoon

    b. A fork

    c. A sewing needle

    d. A crooked pin

14. What does it mean if your ear itches, turns red, and feels hot?

    a. Someone is speaking ill of you

    b. Something bad is going to happen

    c. Someone misses you

    d. You will come into riches

15. What creature is Saint Patrick said to have banished from Ireland?

    a. The lizard

    b. The snake

    c. The hare

    d. The rat

16. What plant is generally considered to be the legendary shamrock?

    a. Clover
    b. Parsley
    c. Watercress
    d. Yellow trefoil

17. Who is the Celtic sun god and god of arts and crafts?

    a. Lugh
    b. Jupiter
    c. Orion
    d. Setanta

18. What is the leprechaun's legendary profession?

    a. Banker
    b. Gardener
    c. Tailor and cobbler
    d. Butler

19. The Fomorians are the evil gods of Irish mythology. Where was their center?

    a. Kilkenny
    b. Dublin
    c. Tory Island
    d. Derry

20. According to an Irish saying, what should you do at a wake?

    a. Drink alcohol
    b. Dance
    c. Wail
    d. Sing

21. **If on a journey you meet a red-haired woman, what should you do?**

  a. Turn back
  b. Cross the road
  c. Take her to dinner
  d. Sing her a song

22. **What is a traditional Irish country cure for chest colds and coughs?**

  a. Carrageen moss simmered in water and lemon juice
  b. Whiskey with hot water and lemon juice
  c. Salt water
  d. A milk bath

23. **What flowering plant was traditionally used for a nerve tonic?**

  a. Daffodil
  b. Nettle
  c. Dandelion
  d. Cowslip

24. **According to Irish folklore, what is believed to cure sore throats?**

  a. Drinking whiskey
  b. Consuming raw eggs
  c. Chewing a clove of garlic
  d. Sucking on the rind of an orange

25. According to tradition, on what day should nobody be without meat?

    a. Shrove Tuesday

    b. Christmas Day

    c. Easter Sunday

    d. Ash Wednesday

26. What kind of weather is welcomed on Good Friday?

    a. Sunny

    b. Snowy

    c. Cold and wet

    d. Windy

27. On what day was it believed that no one should set out on a journey?

    a. Whitsunday

    b. Shrove Tuesday

    c. Ash Wednesday

    d. Good Friday

28. A boy born on what day was destined for high office in the church?

    a. Christmas Eve

    b. Easter Sunday

    c. Saint Patrick's Day

    d. Good Friday

29. **Two people washing their hands at the same basin at the same time are courting what?**

    a. Love

    b. Disaster

    c. Fame

    d. Fortune

30. **In Irish folklore, leprechauns frequently imbibe a special brew given to them by whom?**

    a. The Danes of old

    b. Fairy kin

    c. The devil

    d. Goblins

31. **At a traditional Irish wedding, what is broken over the bride's head for good luck?**

    a. A cracker

    b. A garland of roses

    c. A gold chain

    d. A piece of oatmeal cake

32. **What does the groom throw in the air for good luck upon arriving home with his bride?**

    a. Rice

    b. A bottle of whiskey

    c. The bride

    d. A stack of cards

secrets of
the claddagh ring

The claddagh ring—an internationally recognized symbol of love, loyalty, and friendship—was first created some four hundred years ago in the fishing village of the Claddagh, on the beautiful shores of Galway Bay. A master goldsmith, Richard Joyce, designed and crafted the ring, which depicts two hands clasping a heart, usually topped with a crown.

How the ring is worn conveys information about the wearer. When it appears on the left hand with the heart facing inward toward the body, the ring indicates that the individual is married. Wearing the ring on the right hand in the same fashion suggests that the person is in a relationship or in love. If engaged, one generally wears the ring on the left hand, with the heart pointing away from the body. If one's heart is not yet spoken for, the ring should be worn on the right hand with the heart pointing outward.

33. Breaking a mirror is said to result in how many years of bad luck?

    a. Seven
    b. Twelve
    c. Eight
    d. Two

34. What are the three great festivals of the fairy people?

    a. Spring Solstice, Leap Year, Halloween

    b. April Eve, High Noon, New Year's Eve

    c. May Eve, Midsummer Eve, November Eve

    d. Shrove Tuesday, Christmas, Easter

35. Who is honored on Midsummer Eve?

    a. Setanta

    b. Hy Brasil

    c. Saint John

    d. Saint Peter

36. Who is Turlough Carolan?

    a. The last of the Irish bards

    b. Best friend to the leprechauns

    c. The demon from Shakespeare's *A Midsummer Night's Dream*

    d. A legendary fairy chief

37. What is a changeling?

    a. A unit of measurement

    b. An ugly creature left by fairies in place of a stolen child

    c. A type of musical instrument

    d. An impish demon

38. What does the term *far darrig* refer to?

    a. A type of plant

    b. A ghost

    c. A relative of the leprechaun

    d. A tour guide

39. The cry of what creature is said to herald the death of a member of the listener's family?

    a. Wolf

    b. Banshee

    c. Changeling

    d. Far darrig

40. What can be used as weapons against fairies?

    a. Holy water and bread

    b. Fire and iron

    c. Insults and whiskey

    d. Mistletoe and water

41. In Irish myth, what animal has sacred qualities?

    a. The pig

    b. The rabbit

    c. The frog

    d. The boar

42. What was believed to prevent varicose veins?

    a. Mistletoe

    b. Yellow trefoil

    c. Molasses melted in warm water

    d. Onion grass dipped in vinegar

43. What is the more common name for merrow?

    a. Banshee

    b. Mermaid

    c. Unicorn

    d. Centaur

44. **When a sailor fails to come home, he is sometimes said to have done what?**

    a. Married a mermaid
    b. Slept with the fish
    c. Run with the rum
    d. Danced with the moon

45. **What does the word *selkie* refer to?**

    a. A magical tool
    b. A type of linen tunic
    c. A satyr
    d. A creature that can transform itself from a seal to a human being

46. **What are the banshee's sharp cries and wails called?**

    a. The Lamenting
    b. The Keening
    c. The Piercing
    d. The Shrill

47. **Who wrote the following lines from "The Leprechaun": "A wrinkled, wizen'd, and bearded Elf / Spectacles stuck on his pointed nose / Silver buckles to his hose / Leather apron—shoe in his lap"?**

    a. William Butler Yeats
    b. William Allingham
    c. Samuel Lover
    d. John McGahern

48. What does the word *clurichaun* refer to?

    a. A stag

    b. A large elf

    c. A leprechaun on a drinking spree

    d. An Irish peasant

49. On Saint Patrick's Day, what does a member of the British royal family give to the Irish Guards regiment of the British Army?

    a. A gold coin

    b. A rose

    c. A vial of water from Dublin's River Liffey

    d. A shamrock

50. According to popular mythology, if the leaves of a shamrock are pointing upward, what does this foretell?

    a. Tremendous fortune

    b. Great misfortune

    c. A happy marriage

    d. The coming of a storm

51. What famous warrior of Irish mythology killed the savage hound of Culainn the Smith by slaying it with a hurling stick?

    a. Cúchulainn

    b. Connaught

    c. Gundestrup

    d. Cauldron

52. Which mythological warrior had a hound named Bran, believed to be the original ancestor of the breed known today as Irish wolfhound?

   a. Oisin
   b. Fionn mac Cumhaill
   c. Diarmuid
   d. Cúchulainn

53. According to mythology, what were King Lir's four children turned into by their jealous stepmother?

   a. Swans
   b. Trees
   c. Colors of the rainbow
   d. Teardrops

54. For how long were the children confined in their new forms?

   a. Two weeks
   b. One day
   c. Four hundred years
   d. Nine hundred years

55. Where do fairies live?

   a. In treetops
   b. Under water
   c. Beneath mounds of earth
   d. Under rooftops

56. What form does the legendary Púca (a shape-shifter) most frequently take?

a. A goat
b. A black horse with yellow eyes
c. An eagle
d. A black cat with green eyes

57. What did Saint Patrick purportedly use the shamrock to illustrate?

a. The nature of true love
b. The concept of brotherhood
c. The doctrine of the Holy Trinity
d. The belief system of James II

58. What Irish emblem is featured on the flag of the Island of Montserrat in the Caribbean?

a. The harp
b. The Blarney Stone
c. The Celtic cross
d. The shamrock

59. What does the fictional heroine in William Butler Yeats's play *Cathleen ni Houlihan* inspire young men to do?

a. Travel
b. Lay down their lives for Ireland
c. Hunt leprechauns
d. Sing

60. What is considered Ireland's lucky number?

a. Three
b. Six
c. Five
d. Seven

61. When did Ireland become Christian?

a. In the eighth century CE
b. During the 1950s
c. In the fifth century CE
d. Never

62. What is the origin of the traditional claddagh ring said to be?

a. It was the first ring worn by a mermaid
b. It was created by Richard Joyce as a testament of his love for his wife-to-be during his enslavement to a goldsmith
c. It was given to a mortal by the great claddagh eagle
d. It was a gift from King Claddagh to his mistress

63. According to legend, what did Fionn mac Cumhaill build?

a. Lough Neagh
b. The Giant's Causeway
c. Fingal's Cave
d. Both a and b

64. Why is Chicken's Rock considered to be hazardous to sailors?

a. It was supposedly cursed by Fionn mac Cumhaill
b. It glows luminescent at night, causing sailors to confuse it with the nearby lighthouse
c. It causes sailors to fall ill whenever they pass it
d. It is the home to Gal, an evil mermaid

65. What days in Ireland are called the "Borrowed Days" and are traditionally associated with bad weather?

a. Halloween, Midsummer Eve, New Year's Day
b. March 1, April 1, May 1
c. The first three days in April
d. The fifteenth of every month

66. When was abduction by fairies to be feared most?

a. During the month of May
b. In the month of June
c. On December nights
d. During the full moon

67. What are *immrama*?

a. Magical wands
b. Linen dresses worn by female changelings
c. Tales of sea journeys
d. Mythical creatures that live in lakes

68. **What are the three main manuscript sources for Irish mythology?**

   a. *Book of Kells*, *Red Book of Lecan*, the *Great Book*
   b. *Book of Ballymote*, *Book of Hy Many*, the Cooley manuscript
   c. *Yellow Book of Lecan*, *Book of Leinster*, *Foras Feasa ar Éirinn*
   d. *Lebor na hUidre*, *Book of Leinster*, the Rawlinson manuscripts

69. **Which group was believed to inhabit Ireland before the Gaels?**

   a. The Noahs
   b. The Milesians
   c. The Fomorians
   d. The Tuatha Dé Danann

70. **In Irish mythology, who is the daughter of the Dagda?**

   a. Brighid
   b. Salta
   c. Bres
   d. Roan

chapter 3

City Folk:
Dublin

When I die Dublin will be written in my heart.
—James Joyce

1. What famous river runs through Dublin?

    a. River Liffey
    b. River Laphney
    c. River Lily
    d. River Litney

2. What is Dublin 4 or D4?

    a. A famous Dublin pub
    b. The postal code for an affluent section of Dublin
    c. An artists' collective from the 1970s
    d. A mod-influenced band from the 1960s

3. What is DART an acronym for?

    a. Dublin Art and Resource Training
    b. Dublin Area Rapid Transit
    c. Dublin Area Railway Trade
    d. Dublin Administration Resource Training

4. Which section of Dublin is home to the prestigious Trinity College?

    a. Southeast Dublin

    b. Southwest Dublin

    c. North of the Liffey

    d. None of the above

5. Who built Dublin's Christ Church Cathedral?

    a. The Vikings

    b. The Anglo-Normans

    c. The Romans

    d. The Americans

6. What are the banners and stalls decorated with at Saint Patrick's Cathedral?

    a. The shamrock

    b. The insignia of the Knights of Saint Patrick

    c. The insignia of Adam Loftus, Chancellor of Ireland

    d. The wolfhound

7. What do the sculpted heads on the keystones of the Custom House represent?

    a. Celtic leaders

    b. Great Irish intellectuals

    c. The rivers of Ireland

    d. The towns of Ireland

8. Where is the Old Library located?

    a. North of the Liffey

    b. At the National Gallery of Ireland

    c. At the National Museum of Ireland

    d. At Trinity College Dublin

9. Who holds the Ardagh Chalice, a Celtic Christian treasure dating from 800 CE?

 a. The National Museum of Ireland
 b. The National Gallery of Ireland
 c. The Custom House
 d. Dublin Castle

10. Which building began life as the first purpose-built parliament house in Europe?

 a. The National Library of Ireland
 b. Leinster House
 c. The Mansion House
 d. Bank of Ireland

11. Which building has housed the Irish parliament since 1922?

 a. Leinster House
 b. St. Ann's Church
 c. City Hall
 d. Dublin Castle

12. Who lives in the Mansion House?

 a. Dublin's Chancellor
 b. Dublin's Lord Mayor
 c. Sir Benjamin Guinness
 d. The President of Ireland

13. Who sculpted the artwork *Sphere Within Sphere*, on display on the campus of Trinity College Dublin?

    a. Arnaldo Pomodoro

    b. Paul Koralek

    c. Douglas Hyde

    d. Edmund Burke

14. Trinity College Chapel was the first university chapel in the Republic of Ireland to do what?

    a. Feature a grand organ

    b. Accept donations

    c. Accept all denominations

    d. House temporary art exhibitions

15. Who is believed to have written the *Book of Kells*?

    a. Saint Patrick

    b. The monks of Iona

    c. The monks of Kells

    d. Gerald of Wales

16. What are the Dáil and the Seanad?

    a. The two chambers of the modern Irish parliament

    b. The two wings of the National Library of Ireland

    c. The examination halls of Trinity College Dublin

    d. Popular shopping centers

17. When was Dublin's Age of Elegance?

    a. Nineteenth century

    b. Eighteenth century

    c. Twentieth century

    d. Twelfth century

18. **What has the Powerscourt Townhouse, a beautiful eighteenth-century mansion, been converted into?**

   a. A theater
   b. A restaurant
   c. A shopping center
   d. Luxury condos

19. **A statue of what figure faces the Upper Castle Yard near the main entrance of Dublin Castle?**

   a. William of Orange
   b. Robert Emmet
   c. Justice
   d. Victory

20. **Who was the Hiberno-Norse king of Dublin who originally founded Christ Church Cathedral Dublin?**

   a. Sitric Silkbeard
   b. Blatan Blackheart
   c. Dunan
   d. None of the above

21. **The remains of which historical figure are buried in Christ Church Cathedral Dublin?**

   a. King William III
   b. William of Orange
   c. King James II
   d. Strongbow

22. Where was the Dublin Civic Museum originally located?

a. The Long Hall
b. City Hall
c. The Courthouse
d. City Assembly House

illuminated manuscripts

The oldest surviving Irish manuscripts date from around 600 CE. Scribes in Ireland created their own script and style, inspired by examples from Gaul, Spain, Italy, and North Africa. Trained from an early age, they practiced their art on waxed tablets or slates before turning their hand to creating the ornate, colorful pages that would become their trademark. The most famous and beautiful example of an illuminated manuscript is the *Book of Kells*, which is on view to the public at Trinity College Dublin. Believed to have been brought to Kells by monks fleeing the Viking raids, it contains intricately detailed illustrations of scenes from everyday life that enhance the four Gospels and accompanying text. Exotic colors—yellow ochre, verdigris, and lapis lazuli—make the *Book* unlike any other "book" in existence; it is an inspiring work of art.

23. The casket on the wall of the Chapel of Saint Laud within Christ Church Cathedral Dublin contains the heart of whom?

a. Saint Laud
b. Francis Garthorne
c. Saint Laurence O'Toole
d. Saint Patrick

24. What is the name of Dublin's oldest and only surviving guildhall?

a. Tone Hall
b. Tailors' Hall
c. Wolfe Hall
d. Swift Hall

25. Where did Saint Patrick baptize converts around 450 CE?

a. In the River Liffey
b. In a sacred well next to Saint Patrick's Cathedral
c. In the Wood Quay, an area where the Vikings established their first settlement
d. In his home

26. Which Dublin street was notorious for its brothels in the eighteenth century?

a. Fownes Street
b. Tullow Street
c. Saint Kieran Street
d. Winthrop Street

27. What Dublin building was the center of the 1916 Easter Rising?

a. The General Post Office
b. The Gate Theatre
c. The Custom House
d. The Abbey Theatre

28. How many years did it take to build the monument to Irish statesman Daniel O'Connell, from the laying of its foundation stone in 1864?

a. Two years
b. Five years
c. Nineteen years
d. Two months

29. What is the claim to fame of Dublin's Zoological Gardens?

a. It is the third oldest zoo in the world
b. It was home to the MGM lion
c. It has more howler monkeys than any other establishment
d. Both a and b

30. What is preserved in the vaults of Saint Michan's Church?

a. Gold
b. Caskets of intact bodies
c. Barrels of whiskey
d. Classical caryatids carved by Edward Smyth

31. What is Dublin's busiest thoroughfare?

a. Nassau Street
b. Saint Stephen's Green North
c. Baggot Street
d. O'Connell Street

32. What is the name of the hotel that dominates the north side of Saint Stephen's Green?

a. The W Hotel
b. The Hastings
c. The Shelbourne
d. Londonderry Arms

33. Who is portrayed in the statue at the junction of Grafton Street and Saint Stephen's Green?

a. Henry Moore
b. Molly Malone
c. Charles Stewart Parnell
d. Francis Taylor

34. The statue of Wolfe Tone, the eighteenth-century independence-movement leader, is also known as what?

a. Tarry
b. O'Brien
c. Tonehenge
d. Newton

35. Where is the Lord Mayor's Lounge located?

a. Inside the mayor's house
b. Inside Saint Ann's
c. Inside the Shelbourne hotel
d. Adjacent to the Blarney Stone

36. Which one of the following individuals was a leader of the 1916 Rising?

a. Patrick Pearse
b. Philip Gray
c. Douglas Taft
d. Maire o Ciaragain

37. For whom was the Mansion House built?

a. Peter Hyer
b. Amanda Hague
c. Andrew Hague
d. Joshua Dawson

38. Since 1922, what building has housed the Dáil Éireann—the principal chamber of the Irish parliament?

a. Saint Ann's Church
b. The Mansion House
c. Leinster House
d. The National Library of Ireland

GUINNESS GALORE

While the Guinness Brewery in Dublin is recognized today as Europe's largest producer of beer, sprawling across sixty-five acres, its origins were much more humble. In December 1759, thirty-four-year-old Arthur Guinness was determined to raise the standard of beer. At the time, ale was much criticized. In fact, in rural Ireland, beer was virtually unknown. Instead, whiskey, gin, and poteen were the favored drinks. Aware of a black ale called porter (so called because of its popularity with porters at Billingsgate and Covent Garden), Guinness decided to create his own recipe. Eventually, his brew would become known as stout—and turn into the best-selling alcoholic drink of all time in Ireland.

39. **Saint Ann's Church has a long-standing tradition of charity work. What was Lord Newton's request in this regard?**

　　a. That every parishioner donate time to the poor
　　b. That every parishioner give shoes to the poor
　　c. That every parishioner buy bread for the poor
　　d. That every parishioner wash the feet of the poor

40. What was the English-controlled part of Ireland called from the fourteenth century to the end of the sixteenth century?

    a. The Great Might

    b. The Pale

    c. The Paige

    d. Westminster

41. Where was Handel's "Messiah" performed for the first time?

    a. Musick Hall

    b. Christ Church Cathedral Dublin

    c. Wide Hal

    d. Saint Patrick's Cathedral

42. What is a "Dub"?

    a. A bathtub

    b. A person from either the city or county of Dublin

    c. A type of soap

    d. An Irish breakfast of fried eggs and overripe tomatoes

43. What are the names of the two best cinemas in Dublin?

    a. Savoy and Cineworld

    b. Charleston and Croke

    c. Point and Screen

    d. Temple and Smithfield

44. What venue does the Leinster Rugby team call home?

    a. Parnell Park

    b. Lansdowne Road Stadium

    c. Donnybrook Rugby Ground

    d. Dalymount Park

45. What are the names of Dublin's two canals?

a. The Drogheda and Dundalk
b. The Luas and West
c. The Grand and the Royal
d. None of the above

46. Name Ireland's national broadcaster.

a. Channel 6
b. City Channel
c. Setana Times
d. RTE

47. Who was Catherine Kelly?

a. The first female tennis player
b. The smallest Irish woman ever
c. A fictitious female pirate
d. The first Irish astronaut

48. How many pints of Guinness are produced daily in Dublin?

a. Ten million
b. Five million
c. One million
d. Thirty million

49. Where are the remains of Saint Valentine contained?

a. Phoenix Park
b. Choir Church
c. Whitefriar Street Church
d. Aungier House

50. Where is the first chapter of *Ulysses* set?

a. The National Gallery of Ireland
b. The Martello Tower in Sandycove
c. The Writers' Square
d. The Dubhlinn Gardens

51. What does the plaster relief above the altar in Saint Mary's Pro-Cathedral depict?

a. The Ascension
b. The Fenian cycle
c. The Dubliners
d. The victory of William II

52. What famous building was destroyed by fire in 1921, during the War of Independence?

a. Rothe House
b. Kyteler's Inn
c. The Custom House
d. Kilkenny Castle

53. What does the Garden of Remembrance commemorate?

a. The Viking Invasion
b. The War of Independence
c. The Great Emergency
d. The fiftieth anniversary of the 1916 Easter Rising

54. What did Fergus Mitchell, owner of the first car in Ireland, install outside his home in 1893?

a. A stop sign
b. A traffic light
c. A parking lot
d. A raceway

55. What was O'Connell Bridge originally made of?

a. Wood
b. Concrete
c. Rocks
d. Rope

56. How did the Temple Bar area get its name?

a. It was home to a popular pub built with a roof resembling that of a temple
b. It housed the first Jewish temple built in Ireland
c. It was arbitrarily named
d. It featured Egyptian-like architectural structures

57. What is the claim to fame of Marsh's Library?

a. It contains Europe's largest collection of rare books
b. The bookshelves are made of gold
c. It is Ireland's oldest public library
d. It houses the original *Dubliners* manuscript

58. College Green is a key Dublin landmark. In the past, it served as a Viking meeting place, as well as _____.

a. The seat of Ireland's parliamentary body
b. A burial ground
c. A sacred site
d. A shipping quarter

59. "She died of a fever. No one could relieve her." What famous Dublin fishmonger does this rhyme describe?

a. Molly Malone
b. Molly Brown
c. Daisy Hyde
d. Mary Mack

60. **What pub was the headquarters of Wolfe Tone's Society of United Irishmen?**

   a. The Marsh
   b. 52
   c. The Quay
   d. The Brazen Head

61. **In the spring of 1882, two key British politicians, Lord Cavendish and T. H. Burke, were assassinated by what organization?**

   a. The Invincibles
   b. The Land League
   c. The Hooligans
   d. The County Eight

62. **What famous Dubliner said, "When my country takes her place among the nations of the earth, then and not till then let my epitaph be written"?**

   a. Sir Arthur Guinness
   b. Sinéad O'Connor
   c. Robert Emmet
   d. James Joyce

63. **Of what event in Dublin history was it said, "It is the first time it has happened since Moscow, the first time that a capital has been burnt since then"?**

   a. The accidental bombing of Dublin during World War II
   b. The 1916 Rising
   c. The Irish Civil War
   d. The last Viking raid

64. When is "Bloomsday," the annual celebration of Leopold Bloom's peregrination, as described by James Joyce in *Ulysses*?

    a. June 1
    b. June 16
    c. June 25
    d. June 30

65. What is Dublin's motto, according to its coat of arms?

    a. "Eat, drink, and be merry"
    b. "Never fall, never fail"
    c. "All for one, one for all"
    d. "Happy the city whose citizens obey"

66. Dublin's coat of arms is decorated with three of these:

    a. Shamrocks
    b. Harps
    c. Castles
    d. Tigers

67. Upon whose statue are the words "No man has a right to fix the boundary to the march of a nation" carved?

    a. William Smith O'Brien
    b. Charles Stewart Parnell
    c. Father Theobald Matthew, better known as the Apostle of Temperance
    d. James Larkin

68. Who created the Rotunda Hospital, the first maternity hospital in the British Isles?

    a. Dr. Bartholomew Mosse

    b. Monsignor Hugh O'Flaherty

    c. Thomas John Barnardo

    d. Dr. Robert James Graves

69. Dublin is known for its fanciful and brightly colored doors done in what style of architecture?

    a. Modern

    b. Georgian

    c. French

    d. Greek Revivalist

chapter 4

Genuine Grub and Guinness Galore:
Food and Drink

...the more carrots you chop, the more turnips you slit, the more
murphies you peel, the more onions you cry over... the fiercer the
fire and the longer your spoon and the harder you gruel with more
grease to your elbow the merrier fumes your new Irish stew.
—James Joyce, *Finnegans Wake*

1. Irish stew contains what kind of meat?

    a. Goat
    b. Beef
    c. Lamb
    d. Pork

2. What city is famous for its oysters and oyster festival?

    a. Galway
    b. Belfast
    c. Waterford
    d. Dingle

3. What Irish beverage is traditionally added to a beef stew?

    a. Red wine

    b. Whiskey

    c. Porter

    d. Sloe gin

4. What was traditionally said to cure colds and influenza on chilly days?

    a. Hot whiskey

    b. Bailey's

    c. Tea

    d. Port

5. What teatime dish is traditionally served with jam?

    a. Dry toast

    b. Muffins

    c. Brown bread

    d. Scones

6. What are Ireland's stouts besides Guinness?

    a. Murpheys and Beamish

    b. Murpheys and Blankens

    c. Murpheys and Boynans

    d. Murpheys and Plymouth

7. The traditional Irish Christmas dinner includes what type of fowl?

    a. Pheasant

    b. Goose

    c. Turkey

    d. Quail

8. According to mythology, what did legendary warrior Fionn mac Cumhaill eat to acquire the gift of eternal wisdom?

a. Rabbit
b. Salmon
c. Potatoes
d. Dublin Bay prawns

9. What are Kerr's Pinks, Records, King Edwards, and Golden Wonders?

a. Types of cocktails
b. Names of popular Dublin restaurants
c. Varieties of potatoes
d. Regional names for scallops

10. What is Abrakebabra?

a. Fried steak with a shot of whiskey added to the juice
b. A burger bun baked in batter
c. An Irish fast-food chain
d. Leftover spuds baked with cheese

11. What famous Dublin dish consists of sausages, bacon rashers, onions, potatoes, black pepper, and a rich gravy?

a. Heel overs
b. Bram brack
c. Fadge
d. Coddle

12. When is colcannon traditionally eaten?

a. Halloween

b. Easter

c. New Year's Day

d. Saint Patrick's Day

13. Skirts and kidneys is a dish unique to Cork. What are "skirts" exactly?

a. Trimmings from the spleen

b. Skirt steak

c. Trimmings from pork steaks

d. Thin shavings of rump roast

14. What is choc '99?

a. A hot fudge sundae

b. A soft-serve cone spiked with a Flake chocolate bar

c. A slider

d. A wafer cookie

15. Soda bread is made without which of the following ingredients?

a. Flour

b. Yeast

c. Buttermilk

d. Bread soda

16. What does the "tall blonde in the black dress" refer to?

a. Your date

b. A pint of stout

c. Squeak and bubble

d. A boilermaker

17. What is Smithwicks?

    a. A popular scoop (drink)

    b. The oldest working pub in Kilkenny

    c. A type of gin

    d. Both a and b

18. In addition to the 1980s Miners' Union leader in England, the name Arthur Scargill refers to _____.

    a. A miniaturized bottle of whiskey

    b. A type of cider

    c. Rhyming slang for a gargle (drink)

    d. The hard stuff

19. What is the "fat frog"?

    a. A traditional Easter dish

    b. A two-liter cider

    c. An ATM

    d. A layered mixture of WKD® Blue, Smirnoff® Ice, and Bacardi Breezer® Orange

20. Per capita, the Irish drink more of what beverage than any other nation?

    a. Whiskey

    b. Coffee

    c. Soda

    d. Tea

21. What is "tea you could dance on"?

    a. An awful-tasting cup of tea

    b. An unusually robust cup of tea

    c. A bland form of gravy

    d. An expensive cup of tea

IRISh COffEE

It's been said that only Irish coffee provides all four essential food groups in a single glass: alcohol, caffeine, sugar, and fat. Regardless of whether or not you have a drop of Irish in you, this drink will turn you into a fan of the Emerald Isle.

Ingredients
1 cup hot, strong coffee
1 teaspoon sugar
1 jigger (about 1.5 ounces) of whiskey
1 to 2 teaspoons chilled whipping cream

Warm a whiskey glass with hot water. Add coffee and stir in sugar until dissolved. Add whiskey. Pour the cream over the back of a teaspoon, creating two layers—the whiskey/coffee layer on the bottom and the cream layer on top. Do not mix. Serve promptly.

22. **When making the dish called champ, which of the following ingredients is added to mashed potatoes?**

    a. Garlic
    b. Cabbage
    c. Kale
    d. Scallions

23. What are the five main components of the traditional Irish breakfast?

a. Bacon, colcannon, sausage, egg, fried tomato
b. Bacon, egg, sausage, boxty, fried tomato
c. Boxty, bacon, colcannon, egg, fried tomato
d. Bacon, egg, sausage, black and white pudding, fried tomato

24. What is a Dublin Lawyer?

a. A type of whiskey
b. Lobster cooked in whiskey and cream
c. Soda bread soaked in ale
d. A brand of hot sauce

25. What does the term *fulacht fiadh* refer to?

a. A type of fish
b. An ingredient for mead
c. A site, consisting of a hole in the ground filled with water, for cooking deer
d. A seed used for making porridge

26. What is considered the national dish of Ireland?

a. Corned beef and cabbage
b. Irish stew
c. Soda bread
d. Porridge

27. What is Dublin coddle said to prevent?

a. Hangovers
b. Skin rashes
c. Heartburn
d. Upset stomach

28. What is used to fry the ingredients for haggerty?

 a. Vegetable oil

 b. Olive oil

 c. Butter

 d. Bacon fat

29. What Irish drink specialty was Queen Elizabeth I fond of?

 a. Barley-based whiskey

 b. Stout

 c. Knotgrass tea

 d. Irish Mist

30. What ingredient is used in Scottish whisky but not in Irish whiskey?

 a. Peat

 b. Malted grain

 c. Water

 d. Barley

31. *Praties* is the Irish word for what?

 a. Peas

 b. Spinach

 c. Potatoes

 d. Cabbage

32. What do the Irish call sausages?

 a. Crubeens

 b. Tubies

 c. Links

 d. Bangers

toasts and tipple:
irish drinking sayings

My friends are the best friends,
Loyal, willing, and able.
Now let's get to drinking!
All glasses off the table!

Here's to a long life and a merry one.
A quick death and an easy one.
A pretty girl and an honest one.
A cold pint—and another one!

Here's to a temperance supper,
With water in glasses tall,
And coffee and tea to end with—
And me not there at all!

When money's tight and hard to get,
and your horse is also-ran,
When all you have is a heap of debt,
a pint of plain is your only man.

Here's to being single...
Drinking doubles...
And seeing triple!

I drink to your health when I'm with you,
I drink to your health when I'm alone,
I drink to your health so often,
I'm starting to worry about my own!

Here's to women's kisses,
and to whiskey, amber clear;
Not as sweet as a woman's kiss,
but a darn sight more sincere!

33. What was "souperism"?

    a. The practice of eating a daily bowl of soup

    b. A Catholic's betrayal of his religion by converting to Protestantism in order to receive food from the soup kitchens during the 1800s

    c. The science of finding the perfect bowl of Irish stew

    d. A popular three-day fast during which practitioners eat only tomato soup

34. Tayto, KP Hula Hoops, Walkers, and Hunky Dory are all Irish brands of what?

    a. Candy

    b. Butter

    c. Potato chips

    d. Hot dogs

35. What is dulse?

    a. Edible seaweed

    b. A type of banger

    c. Mashed tomato

    d. Tripe

36. What does the nickname Black and Tans describe (aside from a drink combining pale ale and stout)?

    a. A paramilitary reserve that existed during the Irish War of Independence

    b. Blends of caffeinated and decaffeinated tea

    c. Chocolate-coated caramels

    d. Convertibles

37. What is Cidona?

    a. A type of soda bread

    b. Citrus-infused tea

    c. An apple-based soft drink

    d. A large Irish supermarket

38. What are the two varieties of lemonade in Ireland?

    a. Sweet and sour

    b. Tart and tasty

    c. Red and white

    d. Salty and Ace

39. Taylor Keith, Country Spring, Finches, and Nash's are all brands of what?

    a. Whiskey

    b. Chocolate

    c. Lemonade

    d. Gum

40. Where is Saint Brendan's Irish Cream Liqueur made?

    a. Derry, Northern Ireland

    b. Dublin

    c. London

    d. Belfast

41. What are the two major forms of soda bread?

    a. Square and round

    b. Oblong and triangular

    c. Flat and fat

    d. Loaf and griddle cake

42. In Cork and Limerick, this dish is often paired with tripe for a combination referred to in those areas as "Packet and Tripe." What is the name of the dish?

    a. Drisheen
    b. Tayto
    c. Irish stew
    d. Boxty

43. What is the name of the tangerine-flavored soft drink recently bought out by Coca-Cola?

    a. Tangerino
    b. Orange
    c. Tanora
    d. T-Time

44. What is Veda bread?

    a. A salty soda bread
    b. A malted bread
    c. Sour milk bread
    d. Day-old bread

45. Fill in the blanks in this popular Irish poem: "Boxty on the griddle / Boxty in the _____ / If you can't make boxty / You'll never get _____."

    a. Oven / some lovin'
    b. Dish / your wish
    c. Pan / your man
    d. Tray / your way

46. Who sang the single "The Jumbo Breakfast Roll," which topped the Irish charts in 2006?

a. The Cranberries
b. Thin Lizzy
c. Angela Feeney
d. Pat Shortt

47. In what year was the Kilbeggan Distillery founded?

a. 1857
b. 1757
c. 1957
d. 2007

48. Who invented Irish coffee?

a. Johnny Logan
b. Daniel O'Connell
c. Joseph Sheridan
d. Edward O'Brien

49. What did travel writer Stanton Delaplane convince the Buena Vista Café in San Francisco to start serving on November 10, 1952?

a. Guinness
b. Black and Tans
c. Soda bread
d. Irish coffee

50. Aldi, Centra, Dunnes, and The Cope are all chains of what?

    a. Supermarkets

    b. Liquor stores

    c. Produce stands

    d. Ice cream shops

51. What is traditionally consumed with Christmas pudding?

    a. Rum

    b. Guinness-dipped toffee

    c. Brandy butter

    d. Irish stew

52. Peter the Great, czar of Russia, once said, "Of all the wines, Irish is the best." What beverage was he speaking of?

    a. Merlot

    b. Whiskey

    c. Stout

    d. Porter

53. How many whiskey distilleries were in existence in Ireland during the eighteenth century?

    a. Two thousand

    b. Five hundred

    c. Twelve hundred

    d. Five thousand

54. What is Guinness's main slogan?

    a. "Water, Malt, and Hops"

    b. "Good for You"

    c. "My Goodness, My Guinness"

    d. "It's Guinness Time"

55. Fill in the blank in this popular proverb: "Food is golden in the morning, silver at noon, and _____ at night."

    a. A delight

    b. Lead

    c. Copper

    d. Gone

56. When did the potato arrive in Ireland and where did it come from?

    a. 1580 / South America

    b. 1670 / South America

    c. 1550 / Australia

    d. 1550 / Africa

57. What is potato blight?

    a. A hearty Irish dish that was a staple in the early twentieth century

    b. A fungal disease

    c. A game similar to cricket

    d. An alcoholic beverage made with potato-based vodka

traditional irish stew

Considered one of Ireland's heartiest dishes, Irish stew is also one of the most beloved. What's more, this delicious treat is easy to make.

Ingredients
4 potatoes, thinly sliced
4 onions, thinly sliced
6 carrots, sliced
1 pound Canadian bacon, chopped
3 pounds lamb chops, one-inch thick, trimmed, and cut into small pieces
2 ½ cups water
4 potatoes, halved
fresh parsley, chopped
salt and pepper, to taste

Layer some of the sliced potatoes, onions, and carrots in a stew pot. Follow with a layer of Canadian bacon and lamb. Repeat until all the ingredients are used, except the 4 halved potatoes. Add salt and pepper to taste. Add just enough water to cover those ingredients, then arrange the halved potatoes on top of the stew, but not in contact with the water, so they can steam as the rest of the stew is cooking. Simmer on low for 2 hours. Serve in soup bowl and top with fresh parsley. Makes 4 to 6 servings.

58. What is *The Restaurant*?

  a. A book written in the 1800s describing food preparation techniques in high-end Irish restaurants
  b. An indie movie starring Ewan McGregor and Fiona Shaw as dueling chefs
  c. A successful Irish reality television show
  d. An album by Shane MacGowan

59. Where did celebrity chef Rachel Allen attend school?

  a. The Culinary Institute of America
  b. Ballymaloe Cookery School
  c. Berry Lodge Cookery School
  d. Belle Isle School of Cooking

60. Who is Darina Allen?

  a. Ireland's top food critic
  b. Proprietor of Dublin's most famous and eponymously named restaurant
  c. Ireland's most famous cook
  d. Founder of Ireland's slow-cook movement

61. Which of the following individuals is an Irish food critic who moonlights as an actor?

  a. Paolo Tullio
  b. Georgina Campbell
  c. Caroline Workman
  d. Ciarnan Convery

62. **Douce Mountain Farm in West Cork, Ireland, is an organic farm that also doubles as what?**

    a. A bakery
    b. A bed-and-breakfast
    c. A cooking school
    d. A Zen meditation center

63. **What dish was immortalized in Roddy Doyle's novel *The Van*?**

    a. Ulster fry
    b. Soda farls
    c. Chippers
    d. Oysters

64. **What is Leo Burdock's claim to fame?**

    a. He was Ireland's first food critic
    b. It is Ireland's oldest fish-and-chip shop
    c. He's a famous Irish chef
    d. He opened the first McDonald's in Dublin

65. **Galway salmon consists of salmon, watercress, colcannon, and _____.**

    a. Irish butter sauce
    b. Ham stock
    c. Onions
    d. Crushed walnuts

66. **What fish is considered by the Irish to be a delicacy?**

    a. Cod
    b. Haddock
    c. Whiting
    d. Ray

67. **What small County Cork town has established itself as the "Gourmet Capital of Ireland"?**

    a. Kinsale

    b. Cloyne

    c. Wexford

    d. Waterford

68. **How is a "lady's breakfast" different from a "gentleman's breakfast"?**

    a. The former is served with orange juice

    b. The latter is served with orange juice

    c. A lady's breakfast is served with one egg, while the gentleman's is served with two eggs

    d. There is no difference

69. **What are Carrigaline, Cooleeney, Gubbeen, and Durrus?**

    a. Cheeses

    b. Teas

    c. Soft drinks

    d. Popular Dublin bakeries

chapter 5

The Fighting Irish:
Sports and Games

I'll let the racket do the talking.
—John McEnroe

1. In which sport was Michelle Smith suspended over drug allegations in 1999?

    a. Swimming

    b. Track

    c. Hurling

    d. Gymnastics

2. Which Irish sport is commonly mistaken for the Scottish game of shinty?

    a. Shuffleboard

    b. Hurling

    c. Trekking

    d. Darts

Be sportsmanly

The secret to being a good sports fan is knowing the ins and outs of every game. Equally important is knowing the various figures involved, including the athletes, the referees, and the commentators.

*Match the athlete/sports personality
with the appropriate description:*

A. Packie Bonner
B. Andre Botha
C. Tom Brady
D. Brian Burke
E. Andrew Bree
F. Paul Darragh
G. John Pius Boland
H. Nicky Byrne
I. Michael Carruth
J. Eamonn Coghlan
K. Gordon D'Arcy
L. Ken Doherty
M. Seamus Elliott
N. Mick Galwey

O. Padraig Harrington
P. Eddie Jordon
Q. Elizabeth Hawkins-Whitshed
R. John McEnroe
S. John Doyle
T. Vincent O'Brien
U. Mike McCarthy
V. Mick Doyle
W. Eamon Dunphy
X. Edmond Gibeny
Y. David Finlay
Z. Alan Lewis

1. Rugby referee
2. Footballer
3. Cyclist
4. Rugby player and coach

5. Winner of the World Snooker Championship
6. Cricketer
7. Quarterback
8. Golfer
9. Former Republic of Ireland football manager
10. Boxer (and winner of an Olympic gold medal)
11. Kickboxer
12. Mountaineer
13. Rugby union player
14. Hurler
15. Show jumper
16. Tennis player formerly ranked No. 1 in the world
17. Runner
18. Tennis player
19. Horse trainer (voted the greatest of all time by *Racing Post*)
20. Swimmer
21. Former soccer player, media commentator, and broadcaster
22. Wrestler
23. Footballer—and singer in the band Westlife
24. Equestrian
25. Racecar driver and Formula One team owner
26. General manger of the Anaheim Ducks

Answers: A. 2. B. 6. C. 7. D. 26. E. 20. F. 15. G. 18. H. 23. I. 10. J. 17. K. 13. L. 5. M. 3. N. 4. O. 8. P. 25. Q. 12. R. 16. S. 14. T. 19. U. 9. V. 11. W. 21. X. 24. Y. 22. Z. 1

3. What is Limerick's main rugby venue?

a. Croke Park
b. Thomond Park
c. The Pale
d. Strokestown Park House

4. What Formula One motor-racing team does Eddie Irvine drive for?

a. Ferrari
b. Renault
c. Jaguar
d. Red Bull–Renault

5. What does the G stand for in GAA?

a. Glin
b. Gorey
c. Gaelic
d. Grand

6. Where is the Hogan Stand?

a. Kilkenny
b. Gaelic Grounds
c. Croke Park
d. Kildare

7. For which well-known club did footballer, or soccer player, George Best play?

a. Manchester United
b. Newcastle
c. Irish Youth
d. Stockport County

8. Who is Ireland's top star in the sport of hurling?

    a. Sean Og O'Hailpin

    b. Christy Ring

    c. Nicky Rackard

    d. Ken Hogan

9. Who is Mike Morgan?

    a. Irish National Show Jumper Champion

    b. Irish National Surfing Champion

    c. Irish National Poker Champion

    d. Irish National Chess Champion

10. Which Irish golf course was built between 1987 and 1993 by farmers using hand spades and rakes?

    a. Mount Juliet

    b. K Club's Smurfit Course

    c. Galway Bay

    d. Carne Golf Links

11. What is a sliotar?

    a. A jersey

    b. A golf club

    c. A hurling ball

    d. A hurling goalpost

12. Where is the Irish Derby held?

    a. The Curragh

    b. Fairyhouse

    c. Punchestown

    d. Leopardstown

13. In 2007, Padraig Harrington became the first Irishman since Fred Daly in 1947 to do what?

a. Surf the Irish Sea
b. Win the British Open at Carnoustie
c. Win gold in boxing
d. Qualify to the Super 8 stage of the Cricket World Cup

14. Who designed the golf course at Mount Juliet?

a. Arnold Palmer
b. Christy O'Connor
c. Tiger Woods
d. Jack Nicklaus

15. Ireland has won the most medals in which Olympic sport?

a. Swimming
b. Soccer
c. Boxing
d. Fencing

16. Which sport was introduced to Ireland 1927?

a. Hare coursing
b. Greyhound racing
c. Cricket
d. Irish road bowling

17. When was the Tug of War Association created?

a. 2008
b. 1967
c. 1976
d. 2001

18. What is Coolmore Stud?

a. Term used to refer to a hurling linesman

b. Nickname for boxer Bernard Dunne

c. Award given to master show jumpers

d. The largest thoroughbred racehorse breeding operation

19. What is orienteering?

a. A high-speed car race on an obstacle course

b. A horse race on an obstacle course

c. Synchronized swimming

d. A family of sports that require navigational skills using a map and a compass

20. What is the biggest national sporting event in Ireland?

a. The Community Games

b. The World Cup

c. The All-Ireland Senior Football Championship

d. Swim Ireland

21. How many players are on a Gaelic football team?

a. Four

b. Fifteen

c. Eight

d. Ten

22. Who formed Ireland's first football club, Cliftonville?

a. John M. McAlery

b. Charles W. Alcock

c. Stewart Granger

d. William Bendix

23. When was football introduced to Ireland?

  a. 1776
  b. 1786
  c. 1878
  d. 1898

24. What are Knock, Oldpark, Distillery, Moyola Park, Cliftonville, Avoniel, and Alexander (Limavady)?

  a. Founding clubs of the Irish Football Association
  b. Founding clubs of the GAA
  c. Original names of Irish golf courses
  d. Founding clubs of the Australian Rules Football League of Ireland

25. What sport is believed to predate Christianity?

  a. Football
  b. Hurling
  c. Cricket
  d. Archery

26. What did the GAA ban prohibit?

  a. The playing of foreign games by its members
  b. The consumption of refreshments during matches
  c. Holding games on Sundays
  d. Playing games in Dublin

27. Who created the Surf Club of Ireland?

  a. Tommy Casey
  b. Patrick Kinsella
  c. Roger Steadman
  d. Kevin Cavey

28. In 1994, which Irish runner boasted the fastest time
    of the year in four events—the 1,500 meters, 1 mile,
    2,000 meters, and 3,000 meters?

    a. Fernanda Ribeiro
    b. Gabriela Szabo
    c. Sonia O'Sullivan
    d. Yvonne Murray

29. In what year did James Alexander Porterfield Rynd
    win the first Irish Chess Championship?

    a. 1998
    b. 1800
    c. 1865
    d. 1950

30. After garnering six All-Ireland titles, what did Jack
    Lynch win?

    a. An Academy Award
    b. The position of prime minister
    c. A Grammy Award
    d. The position of head director of the Football
       Association of Ireland (FAI)

31. In what year did Ronnie Delaney win an Olympic
    gold medal for the 1,500 meters?

    a. 1956
    b. 1965
    c. 1900
    d. 1972

32. **An international cycling champion and a former GAA president share the same name. What is it?**

    a. Joe McDonagh

    b. Paul Hession

    c. Trevor Giles

    d. Seán Kelly

33. **Rounders is similar to what American sport?**

    a. Bowling

    b. Baseball

    c. Basketball

    d. Ping-Pong

34. **The Davis Cup and the Fed Cup are international team competitions for what sport?**

    a. Golf

    b. Handball

    c. Tennis

    d. Squash

35. **When was the GAA formed?**

    a. 1923

    b. 1845

    c. 1884

    d. 1950

36. **What hurling position did the mythical hero Cúchulainn play?**

    a. Left corner forward

    b. Goalkeeper

    c. Right halfback

    d. Center halfback

name that team

Showing team affection is a must for any true football fan, and what better way to do so than to bestow a nickname on your favorite team? Whether chiding (in good fun, of course) or cheering, Irish sports lovers are on a first-name basis with their league teams.

Match the FAI Eircom League team name with the correct nickname.

A. Athletic
B. Bohemians
C. Bray Wanderers
D. Cork City
E. Derry City
F. Drogheda United
G. Dublin City FC
H. Dundalk
I. Finn Harps
J. Galway United
K. Longford Town
L. Saint Patrick's
M. Shamrock Rovers
N. Shelbourne
O. Sligo Rovers
P. UCD
Q. Waterford United

1. The Bohs; the Gypos; the Gypsies
2. None
3. The Drogs
4. The Seagulls
5. The Candy Stripes
6. The Harps
7. The Westlanders
8. The Vikings
9. The Craptown
10. De Town
11. The Hoops
12. The Junkies
13. The College
14. The Blues
15. The Real Reds
16. The City
17. Bit O'Red

Answers: A. 2; B. 1; C. 4; D. 16; E. 5; F. 3; G. 8; H. 9; I. 6; J. 7; K. 10; L. 12; M. 11; N. 15; O. 17; P. 13; Q. 14

chapter 6

Invasions, Uprisings, and More:
The Irish Throughout History

People will not look forward to posterity
who never look backward to their ancestors.
—Edmund Burke

1. **What year did Daniel Boone, accompanied by fellow Irish pioneers Major Hugh McGrady and Major James McBride, commence settlement of Kentucky?**

    a. 1775
    b. 1875
    c. 1770
    d. 1645

2. **How many of the original fifty-six signers of the Declaration of Independence were of Irish decent?**

    a. Two
    b. Twelve
    c. One
    d. Eight

3. **Thomas O'Connor published an Irish-American newspaper in what year?**

    a. 1792
    b. 1810
    c. 1805
    d. 1785

4. **What was the name of the newspaper referred to in the previous question?**

    a. *Tammany News*
    b. *Shamrock*
    c. *Saint Patrick*
    d. *Gilgorn*

5. **What is the town of Muckanaghederdauhaulia's claim to fame?**

    a. Ireland's most famous haunted house is located there
    b. Surfing champion Mick Morgan was born there
    c. It boasts the longest geographical name in Ireland
    d. Its name is the origin of the word "muck"

6. **Who was Dame Alice Kyteler?**

    a. The smallest Irish woman in history
    b. Author of *Riders to the Sea*
    c. The last witch in Ireland
    d. Proprietor of Ireland's most famous brothel

7. **What is Saint Fiacre the patron saint of?**

    a. Cooking
    b. Gardening
    c. Gambling
    d. Cleaning

8. Who or what exactly is "the gentleman who pays the rent"?

    a. The man of the house

    b. The landlord

    c. A bill collector

    d. A pig

9. What is "pet day"?

    a. Adoption day at all Irish pounds

    b. A single good day of weather

    c. An all-nighter at the pub

    d. An Irish delicacy

10. What was Dublin's original name?

    a. Dubh Linn

    b. Dubb Lane

    c. Du Blynn

    d. Dybline

11. What entity or city hosted the first Saint Patrick's Day in America?

    a. The Charitable Irish Society of Boston

    b. The Dun Eochla of Boston

    c. Saint Patrick's Cathedral in New York City

    d. Washington, D.C.

12. Who was Grace O'Malley?

    a. Author of the song "Danny Boy"

    b. Commander of a pirate ship during the 1500s

    c. Muse to Jonathan Swift

    d. Famous Irish harpist

13. According to Irish tradition, what should a wedding party do?

a. Drown the shamrock
b. Carry pebbles from Scattery Island in bundled handkerchiefs
c. Take the longest road home from church
d. Celebrate for five days after the wedding

14. What is a *fáinne*?

a. A lapel pin
b. A type of rosary
c. A traditional greeting
d. A type of Irish dessert

15. When did the Act of Union, which united Ireland and Great Britain, come into effect?

a. 1691
b. 1760
c. 1801
d. 1828

16. Despite the fact that the entire island of Ireland had been on the side of the British during World War I, with whom did the newly formed Irish Free State side in World War II?

a. The Allies
b. Japan
c. The Axis powers
d. No one

17. **What was the exact date of the Bloody Sunday in Derry in the 1970s?**

    a. June 30, 1972
    b. January 30, 1971
    c. January 30, 1972
    d. June 30, 1971

18. **What organization also known as the Fenians was founded in 1858?**

    a. The Young Irishmen
    b. The Young Irelanders
    c. The Irish Republican Brotherhood
    d. Sinn Féin

19. **In 1695, many Irish soldiers fled to the Continent. These men became known as what?**

    a. The Wild Geese
    b. The Stalwart Few
    c. Mercenaries
    d. The Lost Exiles

20. **When did Irish women receive the right to vote?**

    a. 1919
    b. 1929
    c. 1939
    d. 1925

21. **When did Ireland join the United Nations?**

    a. 1955
    b. 1952
    c. 1960
    d. 1965

22. What was Irishman John Barry known as?

    a. Father of Ireland

    b. Father of the American Navy

    c. Father of Sinn Féin

    d. Father of the Irish Brotherhood

23. Excavations at Mount Sandel and at Lough Boora have suggested that human beings inhabited Ireland as early as _____.

    a. 3500 BCE

    b. 1014 CE

    c. 9000 BCE

    d. 500 BCE

IRISH VIKINGS?

Vikings settled in Dublin (after raiding it) in the late eighth century. Not only did they build a fort where the River Poddle met the Liffey at a black pool (Dubh Linn) on the current site of Dublin Castle, they also established a settlement along the banks of the Liffey. Following their defeat of Brian Boru, the Vikings integrated with the local Irish population, adopting Christian beliefs. After Strongbow's Anglo-Norman invasion in 1170, the Hiberno-Viking community waned, and many of these people were banished to Oxmanstown, a separate colony north of the River Liffey.

24. **Who is the only leader to have ruled Ireland under one banner?**

    a. Brian Boru
    b. King Cennedi
    c. Saint Malachy
    d. Dermot MacMurrough

25. **What two cities became the capitals of Northern Ireland and the Republic of Ireland, respectively, after partition?**

    a. Cork and Derry
    b. Dublin and Derry
    c. Belfast and Dublin
    d. Belfast and Cork

26. **After partition, Northern Ireland consisted of how many counties?**

    a. Five
    b. Three
    c. Six
    d. Four

27. **The 1998 peace agreement is sometimes referred to as what?**

    a. Holy Thursday Agreement
    b. Easter Sunday Agreement
    c. Good Friday Agreement
    d. Easter Accord

28. The Battle of Clontarf in 1014 marked the decisive defeat of the Vikings. Who led the Irish side?

a. Robert Bruce
b. Brian Boru
c. Strongbow
d. Roger Casement

29. How many men were executed after the 1916 Easter Rising?

a. Fifteen
b. None
c. Twenty
d. Two

30. Which city in Ireland is nicknamed the Maiden City?

a. Derry
b. Cork
c. Dublin
d. Belfast

31. Who was appointed First Minister of the first new Northern Ireland Assembly?

a. Gerry Adams
b. David Trimble
c. John Hume
d. Ian Paisley

32. Who was king of England when the Normans invaded Ireland?

a. Henry I
b. Henry II
c. Henry III
d. Henry IV

33. Which clan retreated from Beara to Leitrim?

a. O'Sullivan
b. O'Henry
c. McCarthy
d. O'Connor

34. In which county did most of the fighting of 1798 take place?

a. Cork
b. Wexford
c. Tipperary
d. Dublin

35. Who led the flying column at Kilmichael in November 1920?

a. Michael Collins
b. Tom Barry
c. Kevin Barry
d. Finn Hurley

36. Who or what killed Michael Collins?

a. Drink
b. Starvation
c. His girlfriend
d. An anti-treaty IRA fighter

37. Which mayor of Cork died on a hunger strike?

a. Tomás Mac Curtain
b. Peter Barry
c. Bobby Sands
d. Terence MacSwiney

38. In what year did the Phoenix Park murders take place?

a. 1982
b. 1882
c. 1828
d. 1928

39. When is it estimated that the Celts reached Ireland?

a. 500 BCE
b. 4000 BCE
c. 300 CE
d. 600 BCE

40. Which Irish saint is said to have discovered America a thousand years before Columbus?

a. Saint Brendan
b. Saint Patrick
c. Saint Angela
d. Saint Christopher

41. In what year did the Irish Civil War break out?

a. 1921
b. 1922
c. 1923
d. 1924

42. **What name was given to the ships that Irish emigrants traveled in?**

    a. Potato ships
    b. Coffin ships
    c. Blarney ships
    d. Dubliners

43. **Where did the potato blight that led to the famine in Ireland originate?**

    a. Ireland
    b. England
    c. The United States
    d. France

44. **When did Viking attacks in Ireland begin?**

    a. 800 CE
    b. 600 CE
    c. 1200 CE
    d. 500 CE

45. **Who, in 1830, was the first Catholic to enter the House of Commons?**

    a. Daniel O'Connell
    b. Robert Emmet
    c. Charles Stewart Parnell
    d. Padraig Pearse

46. **Who first recognized Ireland's independence?**

    a. The United States
    b. Spain
    c. France
    d. England

47. Who was the first woman to be elected to the House of Commons?

    a. Countess Markievicz

    b. Bernadette Devlin

    c. Lady Astor

    d. Margaret Thatcher

48. What famed Irish drink is believed to be the earliest distilled beverage in Europe?

    a. Wine

    b. Ale

    c. Whiskey

    d. Vodka

49. What do Robert Emmet, Charles Stewart Parnell, and Eamon de Valera all have in common?

    a. The were Ireland's first master distillers

    b. They were prisoners in Kilmainham Gaol

    c. They were involved in the Easter Rising

    d. They were exiled to Scotland for their crimes

50. During Dublin's Easter Rising, what were the prison camps called?

    a. Way stations to purgatory

    b. Birdcages

    c. Universities for rebels

    d. Studios for thought

the ORIGIN of halloween

According to old Irish legend, during Samhain—the Celtic New Year—the veil between the material and spirit worlds was very thin. It was believed that the gateway to the otherworld would open and spirits would roam the earth searching for new bodies to possess. During the November 1 celebrations, people would make their homes as inhospitable as possible so that the spirits would be less likely to enter them. All fires were extinguished and people often wore ugly masks and painted their faces grotesquely. This tradition eventually evolved into our Halloween. In the United States, however, Halloween wasn't celebrated until the arrival of the famine-era Irish, who brought with them their eccentric mix of Christian and pre-Christian customs.

51. What is the Senchus Mór?

    a. A black book that contained the names of all rebels

    b. Parliamentary procedure

    c. A bog surrounding Dublin

    d. A collection of civil laws from the fifth century

52. Who introduced coinage to the Irish?

    a. The English

    b. The Vikings

    c. The Swedish

    d. The French

53. In 1151, Dermot MacMurrough kidnapped whose wife?

a. Brian Boru's
b. Adrian IV's
c. Strongbow's
d. Tighearnan O'Rourke's

54. The following lines are from a thirteenth-century poem: "Numerous will be their powerful wiles / Their fetters and their manacles / Numerous their lies, and executions at their stone houses." Who wrote them?

a. King Henry
b. Muirchertach Mac Lochlainn
c. James Clarence Mangan
d. Hugh de Lacy

55. What does the word *caterers* refer to in old Irish?

a. Staff hired to supply a party
b. Professional cattle thieves
c. Castles
d. Singing bards

56. Who was known as "the Proud"?

a. James Butler
b. Roger Mortimer
c. Henry II
d. Shane O'Neill

57. Who said the following words as his only defense during his trial: "From my earliest youth, I have regarded the connection between Ireland and Great Britain as the curse of the Irish nation and felt convinced that, while it lasted, this country could never be free nor happy"?

    a. Oliver Cromwell
    b. Wolfe Tone
    c. Daniel O'Connell
    d. Walter Macken

58. What did Flann O'Brien refer to as a "licensed place of worship"?

    a. A pub
    b. The library
    c. Trinity College Dublin
    d. The theater

59. Who speaks the language of Shelta in Ireland?

    a. The "travelers," a group of gypsy-like individuals who live on the fringe of society
    b. Dublin barkeeps
    c. The Sheltars, a group of farmers in Northern Ireland
    d. The Avatars, a collection of virtual reality–based groups interested in linguistics

60. What is the Cistercian Rule?

a. Belief that monasteries should be more decorative than defensive

b. A rule that monks wash their hands before and after meals

c. The architectural plan for constructing Celtic crosses

d. Rule of motion during legal proceedings

61. What was Dermot McCarthy's claim to fame?

a. He married Elizabeth I

b. He won the Battle of the Boyne

c. He built Blarney Castle

d. He was Ireland's first member of Parliament

62. What is the oldest yacht club in the world?

a. Middleton Club

b. Fota Island Club

c. Cloyne Club

d. Cork Harbour Water Club

63. What did Annie Moore do on January 1, 1892?

a. She became the first woman to sail around Ireland

b. She became the first woman to gain admittance to Trinity College Dublin

c. She was the first immigrant to pass through Ellis Island

d. She swam across the Irish Sea

64. **What is the proper name of the "Nun of Kenmare,"
a woman known for her writings on religious subjects
and social matters during the nineteenth century?**

    a. Mary Francis Cusack
    b. Mary Kerry
    c. Mary Shelley
    d. Mary Saint Michael

65. **Valentia Island, the most westerly point in Ireland,
was chosen as the European end of the first trans-
atlantic cable. What was the first message, sent on
August 5, 1858?**

    a. "Cold. Bring sweaters."
    b. "God Bless each and every one."
    c. "Glory to God and peace on earth to men of
       goodwill."
    d. "May God grant you much happiness and long
       days on this earth."

66. **What do these words by Alfred, Lord Tennyson
describe: "blow, bugle, blow, set the wild echoes flying, /
blow, bugle; answer, echoes, dying, dying, dying"?**

    a. World War II
    b. The Torc Waterfall in Killarney
    c. Fox hunting
    d. The landscape surrounding Dublin

67. **Napoleon's general, Marshal MacMahon, belonged
to a branch of which great Irish family?**

    a. O'Henry
    b. O'Connell
    c. Cennadi
    d. O'Brien

chapter 7

No Time Like the Present:
Ireland Today

What's the use of being Irish if the world doesn't break your heart?
—John F. Kennedy

1. According to Ireland's 2006 census, what was the population of the Republic of Ireland at that time?

    a. 3.5 million
    b. 6.5 million
    c. 10 million
    d. 4.5 million

2. What is Ireland's official color?

    a. Blue
    b. Orange
    c. White
    d. Green

3. How long is the presidential term in Ireland?

    a. Six years
    b. Eight years
    c. Four years
    d. Seven years

4. When was the tricolor recognized as the official flag of the Republic?

    a. 1949

    b. 1937

    c. 1916

    d. 1922

5. Who is the Taoiseach?

    a. The Irish president

    b. The Irish prime minister

    c. Ireland's minister of foreign affairs

    d. Dublin's mayor

6. What is the most common surname in Ireland?

    a. Kelly

    b. O'Sullivan

    c. McCarthy

    d. Murphy

7. What does the prefix "Mac" in Irish family names literally mean?

    a. Son of

    b. Wife of

    c. Brother of

    d. Grandson of

8. What, under the Irish Constitution, is Ireland's first official language?

    a. Irish

    b. Scots Gaelic

    c. English

    d. Celtic

9. On what days are Irish pubs closed?

a. Never
b. Sundays
c. Good Friday and Christmas Day
d. Ash Wednesday and Good Friday

10. Who founded Trinity College?

a. Queen Elizabeth I
b. Walter Raleigh
c. Edmund Spencer
d. William Shakespeare

11. Kissing the stone at Blarney Castle is believed to grant what?

a. Immortality
b. The gift of gab
c. True love
d. Fame and fortune

12. What is the William Clancy Summer School?

a. A school for the deaf in Kilkenny
b. An annual gathering of traditional Irish musicians and dancers from all around the world
c. A dramatic arts school in Belfast
d. A culinary institute in Belfast

13. What is the northernmost county in Ireland?

a. County Limerick
b. County Longford
c. County Donegal
d. County Cavan

14. Which Irish town name means "Ford of the Kings"?

a. Athenry
b. Belfast
c. Leitrim
d. Foxford

15. Which group of islands in Ireland also gives its name to a type of sweater?

a. Rathlin
b. Aran
c. Tory
d. Clare

16. What is the name of the largest park in Dublin?

a. Cashel
b. Mayo
c. Phoenix
d. Wicklow

17. What bridge was recently renovated and is easily one of Dublin's most photographed sights?

a. Ha'penny Bridge
b. Grattan Bridge
c. Millennium Bridge
d. Sean Heuston Bridge

18. What body of water separates the island of Great Britain from Ireland?

a. The Irish Sea
b. The Atlantic Ocean
c. The North Channel
d. St. George's Channel

19. What is the capital of Ireland?

a. Dublin
b. Ulster
c. Belfast
d. Belgrade

20. What is Bertie Ahern's nickname?

a. The Teflon Taoiseach
b. Bertie Bailer
c. Taoisechern
d. Craicie

21. Where was Ireland's president Mary McAleese born?

a. Dublin
b. Paris
c. Rome
d. Belfast

22. When did the Irish government first grant a divorce?

a. 1992
b. 1997
c. 2008
d. 1930

23. What makes Ireland's windmills unique?

a. They are unusually tall
b. They turn in a clockwise direction; the rest of
   the world's windmills turn counterclockwise
c. They are the only windmills in the world to
   be imported
d. They are unusually short

24. What nationality makes up 10 percent of County Roscommon?

    a. Brazilian

    b. French

    c. British

    d. Italian

25. What does "recreational rioting" refer to?

    a. Football

    b. Rugby

    c. Brick throwing between loyalist and nationalist teenagers in mixed Protestant and Catholic areas

    d. Shin kicking between sports fans

26. What is Ireland currently the world's largest exporter of?

    a. Potatoes

    b. Software

    c. Cars

    d. Cell phones

27. How many Americans claim Irish ancestry today?

    a. 10 million

    b. 60 million

    c. Between 25 million and 32 million

    d. Between 40 million and 44 million

28. When is "Little Women's Christmas"?

    a. January 6

    b. December 26

    c. December 31

    d. January 1

all-you-can-eat pancakes

Shrove Tuesday, the day of the annual pancake festival, takes place the day before Ash Wednesday. Before the start of the Lenten fast, over-indulgence is encouraged, with people cooking and consuming mountains and mountains of pancakes. Large, thick pancakes are generally sprinkled with lemon juice and sugar, then rolled up, like cigars. Children and adults alike boast of their pancake-eating accomplishments on Ash Wednesday.

29. What is "Little Women's Christmas"?

   a. A day to celebrate the life and work of Louisa May Alcott
   b. The traditional day for Irish women to ignore their housework
   c. The traditional day of house cleaning
   d. The traditional day to ring in the New Year

30. What name did the town of An Dun recently win the right to change back to?

   a. Fort of the Harlot
   b. Pipes of Yore
   c. Craic
   d. Sister Christian

31. What is Ireland's national symbol?

a. The shamrock
b. The Celtic harp
c. The Blarney Stone
d. The Celtic cross

32. What is the greatest length of the island of Ireland, from north to south?

a. 302 miles
b. 400 miles
c. 502 miles
d. 199 miles

33. Ireland is the _____ island in Europe.

a. Third smallest
b. Third biggest
c. Oldest
d. Youngest

34. The name Ireland is derived from what Celtic goddess name?

a. Ériu
b. Aine
c. Nuada
d. Lugh

35. Who is part owner of the rock venue Eamonn Doran's, located in the Temple Bar?

a. Thin Lizzy's Phil Lynott
b. Eleanor McEvoy
c. Huey Morgan of Fun Lovin' Criminals
d. Moya Brennan

36. Which of the following stores is the most popular among tourists?

    a. Celtic Whiskey Shop
    b. Sheridans Cheesemongers
    c. Butlers Chocolates
    d. Guinness Storehouse

37. What is Arnotts?

    a. Dublin's best-known department store
    b. A fast-food chain
    c. Dublin's most famous pub
    d. A type of soda

38. What county is known as The Kingdom?

    a. Dublin
    b. Waterford
    c. Derry
    d. Kerry

39. Which organization is Ireland *not* a member of?

    a. EU
    b. OECD
    c. UN
    d. NATO

40. How many morning daily newspapers are published in the Republic of Ireland?

    a. One
    b. Two
    c. Three
    d. Four

41. A picture of whom appears on the Irish twenty-pound banknote?

a. William Butler Yeats
b. John F. Kennedy
c. James Joyce
d. Jonathan Swift

42. What is Ireland's international calling code?

a. 353
b. 434
c. 519
d. 915

43. What symbol appears on all Irish coins?

a. The shamrock
b. The Celtic harp
c. The Celtic cross
d. The Irish flag

44. After English and Irish, what language is most widely spoken in Ireland?

a. Russian
b. Swedish
c. Polish
d. French

45. Along with Saint Patrick, who is considered to be a patron saint of Ireland?

a. Saint Nicholas
b. Saint Valentine
c. Saint Bridget
d. Saint Christopher

46. What architectural structure won the prestigious RIBA Stirling Prize?

    a. The Spire of Dublin

    b. The Tall Building

    c. Players Mill

    d. The Elysian

47. How many international airports does Ireland have?

    a. One

    b. Two

    c. Three

    d. Four

48. What is the name of the national airline?

    a. Ryanair

    b. Aer Lingus

    c. Aer Arann

    d. Continental Airlines

49. What is the busiest international air route in Europe?

    a. Madrid to Dublin

    b. Paris to Dublin

    c. London to Dublin

    d. Oslo to Dublin

50. What are the names of the "big four" banks in Ireland?

    a. Allied Irish Banks, Bank of Ireland, National Irish Bank, Ulster Bank

    b. Allied Irish Banks, Suas Bank, De Lorean Irish Bank, Ulster Bank

    c. Allied National Bank, Bank of Ulster, Nation Bank of Ireland, Central Bank

    d. Allied of Ireland, Bank of Ulster, National Bank, Bank of Ireland

51. What is Camara?

    a. A season of fasting

    b. A watchdog community based in Dublin that tracks petty criminals around the world

    c. A charitable organization that sends refurbished computers from Ireland to educational institutions in sub-Saharan Africa

    d. A type of stew made with curry

52. In 2007, Ireland issued a €2 coin for general circulation. What does this coin commemorate?

    a. The 50th anniversary of Sputnik

    b. The 350th birthday of Bernard de Fontenelle

    c. The 40th birthday of Richard Wright

    d. The 50th anniversary of the Treaty of Rome

53. What did the first gold coin issued by the Central Bank commemorate?

    a. The 100th anniversary of Samuel Beckett's birth
    b. The 2nd anniversary of the Special Olympics
    c. The 5th anniversary for the ascension of the ten new European Member union states
    d. The 10th anniversary of the introduction of the euro

54. Irish linen yarn must be spun in Ireland out of what kind of material to be considered 100 percent authentic?

    a. Wool
    b. Flax fibers
    c. Mohair
    d. Alpaca

55. What type of farm does the company Airtricity specialize in?

    a. Tomato
    b. Corn
    c. Potato
    d. Wind

56. How many Airtricity farms are in operation throughout Ireland and England?

    a. Twenty-four
    b. Twelve
    c. Two
    d. Fifty

57. What is Bewley's Grafton Street?

a. A church
b. A café
c. A department store
d. A pub

58. Who designed the series of stained-glass windows at Bewley's Grafton Street?

a. Willie Doherty
b. Alice Maher
c. Harry Clarke
d. Colleen Browning

59. What is the Celtic Tiger?

a. The nickname for Glentoran FC
b. Slang for an exceptionally bad hangover
c. Term used to describe the period of rapid economic growth in the 1990s
d. Annual bagpipe festival

60. What is a drumlin?

a. An elongated whale-shaped hill formed by glacial action
b. A half-pint of Guinness
c. An orange-colored moon
d. A silt deposit

61. What do Cromwell Point, Mizen Head, and Crookhaven all have in common?

    a. They are all breweries

    b. They are all names of lighthouses

    c. They are all famous battle sites in Ireland

    d. They are all famous hotels

62. Which Irish locales have the same names as cities in Africa?

    a. Dublin and Dundalk

    b. Cavan and Brandon

    c. Killarney and Belfast

    d. Baltimore and Ballyhack

63. What is the name of the national park in Northern Ireland?

    a. Mourne Mountains

    b. There is no national park in Northern Ireland

    c. Ballycroy

    d. The Burren

64. Ireland is rumored to have about two hundred crannogs. What is a crannog?

    a. A rare type of wild horse

    b. A labyrinth of mummified remains

    c. An artificial island, used as a settlement

    d. A causeway

chapteR 8

Hopes, Dreams, and Fulfillment:
The Irish in America

*Americans adore me and will go on adoring me
until I say something nice about them.*
—George Bernard Shaw

1. Which U.S. city has the largest number of Irish-Americans?

    a. Detroit
    b. New Orleans
    c. New York
    d. Boston

2. The hand of which Irish-born man wrote the Declaration of Independence?

    a. Henry Adams
    b. George Washington
    c. Andrew Roosevelt
    d. Charles Thomson

3. How many U.S. residents were born in Ireland?

a. 50,000
b. 25,0000
c. More than 1,000,000
d. 130,000

4. What percentage of people living in Massachusetts claim Irish ancestry?

a. 50 percent
b. 40 percent
c. 25 percent
d. 60 percent

5. How many U.S. residents speak Gaelic at home?

a. 10,000
b. 25,000
c. 50,000
d. 100,000

6. Which mayor was of Irish descent?

a. James Duane
b. William Jay Gaynor
c. Thomas F. Gilroy
d. All of the above

7. When was the first Saint Patrick's Day celebration held in Boston?

a. 1876
b. 1857
c. 1737
d. 1767

8. Where is the town of St. Patrick located?

a. Massachusetts
b. New York
c. Missouri
d. Virginia

9. When did Eugene O'Neill win the Nobel Prize in Literature?

a. 1946
b. 1927
c. 1936
d. 1952

10. Which Irish-American boxer held the world heavyweight title from 1916 to 1926?

a. Michael Murphy
b. Jack Dempsey
c. Ryan Sullivan
d. Barry McGuigan

11. Which famous actor was born in Mexico in 1915 to a Mexican mother and an Irish father?

a. Anthony Quinn
b. Barry Fitzgerald
c. John Wayne
d. James Brolin

12. Which native of Kilkenny designed the White House?

a. Frank Lloyd Wright
b. James Hoban
c. James Kelly
d. Louis Sullivan

13. How many places in the United States share the name of Ireland's capital, Dublin?

    a. Seven

    b. Five

    c. Ten

    d. Nine

14. From which New York City building is the Irish flag flown on Saint Patrick's Day?

    a. The Empire State Building

    b. Saint Patrick's Cathedral

    c. City Hall

    d. Carnegie Hall

15. Who was the first Irish mayor of Boston?

    a. Raymond Flynn

    b. James Curley

    c. Hugh O'Brien

    d. John Fitzgerald

16. What does NINA stand for?

    a. No Irish Need Apply

    b. One of Christopher Columbus's ships

    c. New International North America

    d. The tradition of running around the Christmas tree before opening presents

17. What county in Massachusetts boasts the highest number of residents having Irish ancestry?

    a. Middlesex

    b. Norfolk

    c. Nantucket

    d. Suffolk

18. What do Bostonians derisively call potatoes?

a. Murphies
b. McCahans
c. Barrymores
d. Murrays

19. In the 1840s, the Irish made up what percentage of immigrants in the United States?

a. 30 percent
b. 40 percent
c. 50 percent
d. 70 percent

20. Who was the first Irish Catholic to run for President?

a. Al Smith
b. George Washington
c. Andrew Jackson
d. John F. Kennedy

21. What states claim to have the greatest number of people of Irish ancestry?

a. New York, Massachusetts, California
b. Delaware, Massachusetts, New Hampshire
c. Ohio, Massachusetts, Pennsylvania
d. Massachusetts, New York, Virginia

22. How many U.S. presidents have some Irish ancestry?

a. Twenty-seven
b. Eighteen
c. Twenty-two
d. Twenty-three

23. The largest Saint Patrick's Day celebration takes place in New York. Where does the second largest take place?

 a. Boston
 b. Savannah
 c. Charleston
 d. Philadelphia

24. The parents of which American president were both born in Ireland?

 a. Andrew Johnson
 b. William McKinley
 c. James Buchanan
 d. Andrew Jackson

25. Which of the following U.S. presidents have some Irish blood?

 a. Bill Clinton
 b. Grover Cleveland
 c. James Buchanan
 d. All of the above

26. President Barack Obama has Irish ancestry from which county?

 a. County Clare
 b. County Offaly
 c. County Dublin
 d. County Tipperay

the dream fulfilled: the words of john f. kennedy

In 1961, John F. Kennedy became the first Irish-Catholic president of the United States of America. He was the great-grandson of Irish immigrants who hailed from the County Limerick village of Bruff, in western Ireland. Relishing his heritage, President Kennedy spoke fondly of the Irish character and spirit.

When my great-grandfather left [Ireland] to become a cooper in East Boston, he carried nothing with him except two things: a strong religious faith and a strong desire for liberty. I am glad to say that all of his great-grandchildren have valued that inheritance.

The White House was designed by Hoban, a noted Irish-American architect, and I have no doubt that he believed by incorporating several features of the Dublin style he would make it more homelike for any president of Irish descent. It was a long wait, but I appreciate his efforts.

All of us of Irish descent are bound together by the ties that come from a common experience; experience which may exist only in memories and in legend but which is real enough to those who possess it.

27. **Which U.S. cities have had more mayors of Irish descent than of any other background?**

   a. New York, San Francisco, Chicago
   b. Boston, Houston, Philadelphia
   c. Chicago, Boston, Jersey City
   d. Boston, New York, Newark

28. **The Know Nothing Party originated in New York in what year?**

   a. 1849
   b. 1843
   c. 1850
   d. 1855

29. **Who does the term "Plastic Paddy" refer to?**

   a. Someone of Irish heritage who was not born in Ireland
   b. A person who emigrated from Ireland to the United States
   c. A person who has moved to Ireland from the United States
   d. A person who was not born in Ireland and who has no Irish ancestry

30. **What was notorious Irish-American Billy the Kid's real name?**

   a. William McManus
   b. Billy Fitzgerald
   c. William Bonney
   d. Bill Connor

31. What did Bostonians once call their Irish female servants?

    a. "Biddys"
    b. "Paddys"
    c. "Murphys"
    d. "Marys"

32. The "Molly Maguires" were miners who organized into a union in the 1860s and 1870s. What was their union called?

    a. Workingmen's Benevolent Association
    b. Association for Miners
    c. Benevolent Association for Miners
    d. Miners' National Association

33. Who piloted the first transatlantic, nonstop flight from the United States to Ireland?

    a. Amelia Earhart
    b. Charles Lindbergh
    c. Amy Johnson
    d. John Alcock and Arthur Brown

34. Which Irish native was hanged in Boston in 1688 on accusations of being a witch?

    a. Annie Glover
    b. Sarah Osbourne
    c. Martha Cory
    d. Dorothy Good

35. In which city were the Abbey Players arrested and charged with performing plays of an immoral nature?

    a. Chicago

    b. Savannah

    c. Boston

    d. Philadelphia

36. Who "invented" the American department store and is quoted as saying, "You must never actually cheat the customer, even if you can. You must make her happy and satisfied, so she will come back"?

    a. John Wanamaker

    b. Rowland Hussey Macy

    c. Alexander Turney Stewart

    d. William Russell Grace

37. Who founded the *Irish World* in New York in 1870 and edited it until his death in 1913?

    a. John O'Hara

    b. Flann O'Brien

    c. Patrick Ford

    d. Brendan Ford

38. Who captured the British schooner *Margaretta* in Machias Bay, Maine, on June 12, 1775, in the first naval battle of the American Revolution?

    a. Jeremiah O'Brien

    b. Benjamin Foster

    c. Jonathan Haraden

    d. Joshua Barney

39. **Who earned the nickname "Cinderella Man" for his amazing boxing comeback?**

    a. Tuffy Griffiths
    b. James J. Jefferies
    c. James J. Corbett
    d. James J. Braddock

40. **When denounced on the Senate floor as the "grandmother of all agitators," this woman replied, in typical fashion, "I hope to live long enough to be the great-grandmother of all agitators." Who is she?**

    a. Mother Margaret
    b. Mother Jones
    c. Mother Harris
    d. Mother Catherine

41. **Who founded Boys Town?**

    a. Father Patrick Sullivan
    b. Father Michael C. Kelly
    c. Father Edward J. Flanagan
    d. Father Sean Dobbins

42. **What film version of a classic American novel was shot in Ireland, with Gregory Peck as the star?**

    a. *The Quiet Man*
    b. *Moby Dick*
    c. *The Great Gatsby*
    d. *Ryan's Daughter*

43. **Which town in County Tipperary is home to the Ronald Reagan Bar?**

   a. Clonmel
   b. Ballyporeen
   c. Nenagh
   d. Mayo

44. **In what year did President John F. Kennedy visit Ireland?**

   a. 1961
   b. 1962
   c. 1963
   d. 1964

45. **During his visit to Wexford, Ireland, what did President Kennedy place at the John Barry statue?**

   a. A flower
   b. A wreath
   c. A picture
   d. A medal

46. **On May 1, 1933, during the depths of the Great Depression, the *Catholic Worker* newspaper made its debut with a printing of 2,500 copies. Dorothy Day and a few others hawked the paper in New York's Union Square for a penny a copy. How much does the paper cost today?**

   a. Twenty-five cents
   b. One dollar
   c. Fifty cents
   d. One penny

47. John Huston directed which of the following films?

    a. *The Maltese Falcon*

    b. *Moby Dick*

    c. *The Treasure of the Sierra Madre*

    d. All of the above

48. How many championships has Notre Dame won as of the spring of 2008 (in both men's and women's sports)?

    a. Thirty-five

    b. Twenty-five

    c. Thirty

    d. Forty

49. What gang in Boston was one of the most successful organized-crime groups in American history?

    a. The Seven Group

    b. The Westies

    c. The Winter Hill Gang

    d. The K&A Gang

50. What color has been long associated with Saint Patrick?

    a. Blue

    b. Green

    c. Yellow

    d. Orange

chapter 9

Who Said What?
Quotable Quotes

*In Ireland, the inevitable never happens
and the unexpected constantly occurs.*
—Sir John Pentland Mahaffy

1. Who said, "Actually I'm a drinker with writing problems"?

    a. Flannery O'Connor
    b. Frank McCourt
    c. Brendan Behan
    d. Thomas Moore

2. Who called Guinness the "wine of Ireland"?

    a. David Letterman
    b. James Joyce
    c. Andy Warhol
    d. Humphrey Bogart

3. Who wrote, "I said the thing which was not"?

    a. William Butler Yeats
    b. Jonathan Swift
    c. Eugene O'Neill
    d. William Kennedy

4. Which football superstar said, "I spent 90 percent of my money on women and drink. The rest I wasted"?

  a. George Best
  b. Roy Keane
  c. Rio Ferdinand
  d. Pat Jennings

5. Which world leader said, "We have always found the Irish a bit odd. They refuse to be English"?

  a. Queen Elizabeth
  b. Tony Blair
  c. Theodore Roosevelt
  d. Winston Churchill

6. Which leader said, "I tell you this—early morning I signed my death warrant"?

  a. Charles J. Haughey
  b. Michael Collins
  c. Ian Paisley
  d. Eamon de Valera

7. Which Irish writer said, "When anyone asks me about the Irish character, I say look at the trees. Maimed, stark, and misshapen, but ferociously tenacious"?

  a. James Joyce
  b. Nuala O'Faolain
  c. Edna O'Brien
  d. Frank McCourt

8. **Which famous dramatist wrote, "An Irishman's heart is nothing but his imagination"?**

   a. Tennessee Williams
   b. George Bernard Shaw
   c. Sam Shephard
   d. Dylan Thomas

9. **A fan of Sean O'Faolain's literary works wrote him a letter that read, "I hear that your writing yields you a retail price of $1.00 per word. I enclose $1.00, for which please send me a sample." What was the author's one-word response?**

   a. "No"
   b. "Hello"
   c. "Love"
   d. "Thanks"

10. **George Bernard Shaw once received an invitation that read, "Lady Tillingham-Swarthmore will be at home Thursday between four and six." How did he respond?**

    a. He visited Lady Swathmore at five in the evening
    b. He sent a reply that read, "Mr. George Bernard Shaw likewise"
    c. He sent a note that read, "I may never write again"
    d. He wrote the short story "Lady Swarthmore's Soiree"

11. The Claddagh Gypsies of Galway have a saying: "Gypsy gold does not chink and glitter. It gleams in the sun and ____ in the dark."

    a. Glows

    b. Sparkles

    c. Neighs

    d. Sings

12. Which American poet wrote, "The Irish have the thickest ankles in the world / and the best complexions"?

    a. John Berryman

    b. Sylvia Plath

    c. e. e. cummings

    d. T. S. Eliot

13. Who wrote the following as part of an open letter from a Field Day Pamphlet rebuking the editors of the *Penguin Book of Contemporary British Poetry* for including him among its authors?

"Don't be surprised / If I demur, for, be advised / My passport's green. / No glass of ours was ever raised / To toast the Queen."

    a. George Bernard Shaw

    b. Shane MacGowan

    c. Seamus Heaney

    d. Sean O'Casey

wilde wit:
the memorable words
of oscar wilde

*Complete the Oscar Wilde quotes with
the appropriate word from below.*

A. No man is rich enough to buy back his _____.

B. Good _____ are simply checks that men draw
on a bank where they have no account.

C. Men become old, but they never become _____.

D. Crying is the refuge of plain women, but the
ruin of ____ ones.

E. Women are meant to be _____, not to be
understood.

F. I prefer women with a past. They're always so
damned _____ to talk to.

G. The ____ have an insatiable curiosity to know
everything, except what is worth knowing.

H. _____ is much too important a thing ever to
talk seriously about.

I. Life is never _____, and perhaps it is a good
thing for most of us that it is not.

J. A _____ may ruin a human life.

1. resolutions	6. past
2. loved	7. fair
3. amusing	8. kiss
4. pretty	9. life
5. good	10. public

Answers: A. 6; B. 1; C. 5; D. 4; E. 2; F. 3; G. 10; H. 9; I. 7; J. 8

14. Who said, "From the depths of my heart I believe Northern Ireland has come to a time of peace, a time when hate will no longer rule"?

    a. Ian Paisley
    b. Martin McGuinness
    c. Bertie Ahern
    d. Rotimi Adebari

15. Fill in the missing word in this quote from Oscar Wilde: "We can have in life but one great experience at best, and the secret of life is to _____ that experience as much as possible."

    a. Cherish
    b. Reproduce
    c. Celebrate
    d. Share

16. Which Nobel Peace Prize winner said, "When people are divided, the only solution is agreement"?

    a. Samuel Beckett
    b. Seán MacBride
    c. David Trimble
    d. John Hume

17. Which GAA president said, "I have rarely been prouder or more conscious of my country and my nationality," in reference to the historic Ireland versus England rugby match at Croke Park?

    a. Sean Kelly
    b. Peter Quinn
    c. Joe McDonagh
    d. John Dowling

18. What literary figure said, "Our Irish blunders are never blunders of the heart"?

a. Oscar Wilde
b. Douglas Hyde
c. Maria Edgeworth
d. Brian Friel

19. Who said, "I just dress up what the Good Lord provides"?

a. T. E. Kalem
b. Dorothy Macardle
c. Eddie Hackett
d. Brendan Behan

20. To what does the above quote refer?

a. The Ring of Kerry golf course
b. The inspiration behind *The Uninvited*
c. A theater review of *Borstal Boy*
d. An outfit worn to the Irish Film Festival

21. Which U.S. president said, "Ireland, thou friend of my country in my country's most friendless days, much injured, much enduring land, accept this poor tribute from one who esteems thy worth, and mourns thy desolation"?

a. John F. Kennedy
b. John Adams
c. George Washington
d. James Monroe

22. **Which work by Mary Higgins Clark does the following quote come from: "All her life she was to personify the best of her Irish heritage—a generous heart, faith in her God, unswerving allegiance to the Democratic Party, heroic resiliency in trouble and always, always, an unquenchable sense of humor"?**

 a. "My Wild Irish Mother"
 b. *Daddy's Little Girl*
 c. *My Gal Sunday*
 d. *No Place Like Home*

23. **Which associate of Oscar Wilde said, while testifying at the writer's trial, "I think people should be allowed to do what they want, as long as they don't do it in the street and frighten the horses"?**

 a. His doctor
 b. His cleaning lady
 c. His dog walker
 d. His neighbor

24. **Who said, "Love is never defeated, and I could add, the history of Ireland proves it"?**

 a. Liam O'Flaherty
 b. Pope John Paul II
 c. Thomas Moore
 d. John Stuart Mill

25. **Which U.S. president said, "My Ulster blood is my most priceless heritage"?**

 a. Andrew Jackson
 b. John F. Kennedy
 c. James Buchanan
 d. Ronald Reagan

26. **Which American poet ends the poem "Spenser's Ireland" with these words: "I am troubled, I'm dissatisfied, I'm Irish"?**

   a. Galway Kinnell
   b. Marianne Moore
   c. Wallace Stevens
   d. John Berryman

27. **To which New York mayor did Franklin D. Roosevelt address the question, "Why do you Irish always answer a question with a question"?**

   a. John Lindsay
   b. Jimmy Walker
   c. Fiorello La Guardia
   d. Al Smith

28. **Who wrote, "Ah, we men and women are like ropes drawn tight with strain that pull us in different directions"?**

   a. Samuel Lover
   b. C. S. Lewis
   c. Oliver Goldsmith
   d. Bram Stoker

29. **What did Samuel Butler compare praise to?**

   a. The fleeting sound of distant drums
   b. Gold and diamonds, who owe their value only to their scarcity
   c. A child's intellect
   d. The richest treasure in the world

30. **Who wrote, during her visit to Ireland, "It is a lovely country, but very melancholy, except that people never stop talking"?**

   a. Queen Victoria
   b. Marianne Moore
   c. Virginia Woolf
   d. Iris Murdoch

31. **Fill in the blanks in the following quote from Thomas Otway: "Saint Patrick stood bell in hand, and every time he rang it flung away from him . . . and every time it thus hastily was rung, thousands of_____, _____, and _____ things went down, tumbling necks and heels one after the other."**

   a. snakes, beetles, crawling
   b. toads, adders, noisome
   c. mice, cats, quarreling
   d. lizards, snails, slimy

32. **Which of the following lines from William Butler Yeats were inscribed on a stone of Thoor Ballylee?**

   a. "Here, traveler, scholar, poet, take your stand..."
   b. "The trees are in their autumn beauty..."
   c. "I, the poet William Yeats / With old millboards and sea-green slates..."
   d. "The stone-mason was awfully good at drip-stones..."

33. **Who is the subject of W. Mulchinock's poem containing the lines, "She was fair as the rose of the summer / Yet 'twas not her beauty alone that won me"?**

    a. Queen Elizabeth I
    b. Molly Malone
    c. Mary, the Rose of Tralee
    d. Elizabeth Price

34. **Who famously said, "No man is an Ireland"?**

    a. Ronald Reagan
    b. John F. Kennedy
    c. Chicago mayor Richard Daley
    d. New York mayor Michael Bloomberg

35. **Who said, "I always like to know everything about my new friends, and nothing about my old ones"?**

    a. Oscar Wilde
    b. Roddy Doyle
    c. Samuel Beckett
    d. Edna O'Brien

36. **Graham Norton once said that he didn't think he had bad taste. What did he think he *did* have?**

    a. Style
    b. Substance
    c. Talent
    d. No taste

37. Who said, "Music can change the world because it can change people"?

    a. Bono
    b. The Edge
    c. Enya
    d. Van Morrison

38. From what film is the line "All is nothing, therefore nothing must end"?

    a. *Cinderella Man*
    b. *My Left Foot*
    c. *Michael Collins*
    d. *The Pretenders*

39. Whom was William Butler Yeats talking about when he said, "Never have I encountered so much pretension with so little to show for it"?

    a. James Joyce
    b. Oscar Wilde
    c. Samuel Becket
    d. Jonathan Swift

40. To whom was Oscar Wilde referring when he said, "[He] hasn't an enemy in the world, but none of his friends like him"?

    a. James Joyce
    b. William Butler Yeats
    c. George Bernard Shaw
    d. Brendan Behan

41. When Brendan Behan was asked why he hadn't considered a life of sobriety, what was his answer?

   a. "Society should only exist to make the roads better and the drinks stronger. Since I don't know anything about road-building, I'll stick to drinking."
   b. "Because the price of a pint of orange juice is twice the price of a pint of stout."
   c. "That which doesn't kill you only makes you stronger."
   d. "I've never been a quitter before in my life. I don't want to start now."

42. In 1907, the word *shift* (a woman's undergarment) caused an uproar when uttered during a play by John Millington Synge, starring Lady Gregory. The actress asked William Butler Yeats what she should do in response to the hullabaloo. What was his reply?

   a. "Leave it on."
   b. "Take it off."
   c. "Stumble the line."
   d. "Leave acting and sell lingerie."

43. What were Brendan Behan's last words?

   a. "I should have never switched from rum to whiskey."
   b. "It's curtains for me."
   c. "I never got to punch Joyce."
   d. "Thank you, Sister, and may you be the mother of a bishop."

44. George Bernard Shaw sent Winston Churchill two tickets to the opening of his play, along with a note that read, "Bring a friend, if you have one." What was Churchill's reply?

    a. "I'll bring an enemy instead."

    b. "Does my wife count?"

    c. He returned the tickets with a note saying, "Could I have tickets for the second night—if there is one?"

    d. "Between the two of us, we seem to know everyone there is to know—no one!"

45. What play is the following quote from: "Though I should mingle with the dust, or fall to ashes in flame, the plough will always remain to furrow the earth, the stars will always be there to unveil the beauty of the night…"?

    a. *Pygmalion*

    b. *Windfalls*

    c. *Under a Colored Cap*

    d. *Drums Under the Window*

46. Who wrote the play discussed above?

    a. Sean O'Casey

    b. William Butler Yeats

    c. George Bernard Shaw

    d. Samuel Beckett

47. To whom did Maud Gonne write, "The world should thank me for not marrying you"?

    a. Oscar Wilde

    b. John Millington Synge

    c. George Bernard Shaw

    d. William Butler Yeats

48. Complete the wedding toast "Here's to our wives and girlfriends":

    a. May they never meet!

    b. May they live long and prosper!

    c. May they have favor on their side!

    d. May they forgive us!

49. Who said the following: "Being Irish is very much a part of who I am. I take it everywhere with me."

    a. Bono

    b. James Boswell

    c. Sean Connery

    d. Colin Farrell

50. What did Iris Murdoch compare being Irish to?

    a. Being a woman: "Everyone says you're important and nice, but you take second place all the time."

    b. Being poor: "Everyone says you're going to go far, but you get soup while others get steak."

    c. Being happy: "Everyone says you're a merry folk, and that may be so!"

    d. Being lucky: "Everyone says it's their lucky day, but the Irish are born lucky."

chapter 10

But What Does It Mean?
Irish Words and Phrases

For an Irishman, talking is a dance.
—Deborah Love

1. What does "flight of earls" connote?

    a. A type of Irish dance
    b. The events of 1607, when the Earl of Tyrone went into exile, taking other lords with him
    c. A term used to describe all those who left Ireland in the seventeenth century
    d. A popular song from the 1980s

2. According to myth, what did Saint Patrick say when he drove the snakes out of Ireland?

    a. "To hell or Connaught!"
    b. "Join the wild geese"
    c. "Are youse all right in the back there, lads?"
    d. "Slán" (good-bye)

3. What word is an anglicization of the ancient Gaelic *uisce beatha*, which translates as "water of life"?

    a. Whiskey

    b. Mead

    c. Beer

    d. Poteen

4. What does "real Dublin" refer to?

    a. Irish immigrants

    b. Things that are traditional and usually pretty rough

    c. A person who is very Irish

    d. Those who emigrated from Ireland after the potato crop famine

5. Which of the following is synonymous with "so-so"?

    a. "I am in me wick"

    b. "Middling"

    c. "Definitely maybe"

    d. "No spring chicken"

6. What does the word *seanchai* refer to?

    a. A high-ranking Irish militant

    b. A storyteller

    c. A type of tea

    d. A type of inlet

7. What does "a few gargles on ye" mean?

    a. A few drinks

    b. A bit of money

    c. A headache

    d. A bad sense of direction

8. If you have a "buzzer," what do you have?

  a. A haircut
  b. A massage tool
  c. A doorbell
  d. A bee sting

9. What is slang for a bald person?

  a. "Gatch"
  b. "Ronnie"
  c. "Scaldy"
  d. "Smig"

10. According to legend, after a furious argument between two earls in Dublin's Saint Patrick's Cathedral, one earl barricaded himself in a room and the other "chanced his arm." What exactly did the second earl do?

  a. Boxed down the door
  b. Cut a hole in the door, stuck his arm through, and invited his rival to shake hands
  c. Wrote a message of apology on his arm
  d. Wrapped a piece of white linen on his arm to show his surrender

11. What are "blutchers"?

  a. Pot lids
  b. A collection of saws
  c. Heavy boots
  d. A gaggle of geese

12. What is a "brat"?

a. A spoiled child
b. A cloak
c. A broach
d. A magnifying glass

13. What is the colloquial meaning of "riverdance"?

a. To skip to an upbeat tempo
b. To commit suicide in the Shannon River
c. To knit
d. To forgive the ancestors of someone who's wronged you

14. According to Irish street slang, what do the terms "ball hoppers," "bluebottles," "bizzies, "mules," "peelers," "shades," and "razzers" describe?

a. The police
b. Sunglasses
c. Cars
d. Criminals

15. Who coined the phrase "the demon drink"?

a. Arthur Scargill
b. Edward Carson
c. King Billy
d. Father Matthew Theobald

16. What is the "angel's share"?

a. A type of Celtic cross

b. The traditional belief that for every euro earned, a percentage should go to the church

c. The whiskey that evaporates from the barrels during the maturation period of five to twelve years

d. A special prayer held over several days to a particular saint or deity

17. What is the difference between a Baby Guinness and a Johnny Jump Up?

a. A Johnny Jump Up doesn't contain Guinness

b. A Baby Guinness is a small glass of beer; a Johnny Jump Up is a large one

c. A Baby Guinness mixes Bailey's and Guinness; a Johnny Jump Up mixes Guinness and cider

d. A Baby Guinness doesn't contain alcohol, while a Johnny Jump Up does

18. What is "Paddy's eyewater" a colloquialism for?

a. Poteen

b. Whiskey from Munster

c. Half ale and half stout

d. Dirty water

19. The word *hooligan* comes from the name of which famous Irish family in London in the 1890s?

a. The Hoopers

b. The Houlihans

c. The Horgans

d. The McCarthys

that beats banagher: colloquial expressions

The town of Banagher in Offaly was known as a "pocket borough" by the old Irish parliamentary body, meaning the electorate was small enough to be under the effective control (or in the pocket) of one major landowner, the local lord. The town became synonymous for this once-common—and corrupt—way of conducting politics, so if something was really anomalous, it was said to "beat Banagher." While the Irish have an expression for just about everything and every situation, the challenge is to say that something "beats Banagher" ("that's the best I've heard yet").

Match the expressions with the proper translation.

A. Dry up.
B. I am in me wick.
C. Luvly hurdling.
D. You have your glue.
E. You're like the police.
F. Well, boy.
G. Let the dog see the rabbit.
H. Keep your breath to cool your porridge.
I. I was stung.
J. Pull your socks up.

1. Don't be silly.
2. You're never where you're wanted.
3. Get to work.
4. I was embarrassed.
5. Shut up.
6. You must be joking.
7. Great job.
8. Stop wasting your time talking to me.
9. Show it to me and then I'll understand.
10. Hello.

Answers: A, 5; B, 6; C, 7; D, 1; E, 2; F, 10; G, 9; H, 8; I, 4; J, 3

20. If someone says, "Get on side," what are they asking you to do?

a. Move indoors
b. Get lost
c. Behave yourself
d. Shut up

21. What does the phrase *Erin go bragh* mean?

a. "Go, team, go!"
b. "Ireland forever"
c. "Ireland the great"
d. "Ireland the brave"

22. If you enjoy having a bit of *craic*, what do you like to do?

a. Have fun
b. Play football
c. Dance an Irish jig
d. Sing

23. If you are "getting the messages," what are you doing?

a. Working as a secretary
b. Breaking up with your spouse
c. Going grocery shopping
d. Betting on horses

24. What is "Irish beauty"?

a. Outstanding good looks
b. Impressive intelligence
c. Two black eyes
d. A famous Irish racehorse

25. What does "on the pig's back" mean?

a. Good fortune
b. Drunk
c. Overeating
d. Smelly

26. If you are going to work in the *marra*, when do you have to be there?

a. Tuesday
b. Tomorrow
c. Next week
d. Friday

27. What does the slang word "ronnie" mean?

a. Red
b. Fist
c. Moustache
d. Goatee

28. The slang word mentioned above is based on the name of which individual?

a. Ronald Colman
b. Charles Boycott
c. Ronald Reagan
d. Thomas Francis Meagher

29. If someone is described as "maggalore," this person is:

a. Drunk
b. Upset
c. Annoying
d. Wealthy

30. In modern Ireland, which of the following descriptions is one definition for the word *publican*?

    a. A person who runs a saloon or inn
    b. Someone who frequents pubs
    c. Someone who is a friend of the people
    d. A type of Irish dance

31. What are the giant deer that initially roamed Ireland called?

    a. Maximule
    b. Megladeer
    c. Megaceros
    d. Dorma

32. In ancient times, after a deceased person was buried, stones were heaped over the grave. What was this pile of stones called?

    a. Cinterary
    b. Chamers
    c. A cairn
    d. Tara

33. Only about fifty of the old Norse words found their way into common Irish usage. Which of the following made the cut?

    a. Bad
    b. Stuir
    c. Hennypenny
    d. Both a and b

34. President John F. Kennedy's ancestors were Irish. What is his ancestral last name?

    a. Cennedi

    b. Canardi

    c. Kenidi

    d. Cinidey

35. What is *airneál*?

    a. A traditional Irish music session

    b. The Irish tradition of an evening spent with storytelling by the fire

    c. A relaxed party atmosphere

    d. A traditional Irish dance session

36. Which of the following is the correct way to use the word *quern*?

    a. I'm *quern* tired.

    b. The devil's *quern* to ya!

    c. That is a *quern* car.

    d. In the morning, I'm very *quern*.

37. Jack Russell is a type of dog, but what does the Irish slang *Jack Russells* mean?

    a. Type of drink

    b. Hung over

    c. Muscles

    d. Oysters

38. Who first used the term "Paddy" to refer to the Irish?

    a. The Swedish

    b. The Americans

    c. The Irish

    d. The Norse

39. Which of the following accurately describes a *pruheen*?

    a. A hairstyle from the 1950s

    b. A Christmas wreath

    c. A small amount of porridge

    d. A small house or cabin

40. In the United States, children need to do homework for school. What is the equivalent slang word in Irish?

    a. Scratcher

    b. Mollie

    c. Ecker

    d. Cog

41. What do students shout when a fight breaks out in the schoolyard?

    a. "Milly up!"

    b. "Scrap!"

    c. "Tear up!"

    d. "Fight!"

42. What do the terms "slider" and "thatch" refer to?

    a. A type of burger

    b. A moustache

    c. A wig

    d. An insult

43. The Irish refer to gum boots as _____.

    a. Rushers

    b. Wellies

    c. Mints

    d. Both a and b

44. If someone lives in a *knackeragua*, where do they live?

    a. Ulster

    b. A rough area

    c. Dublin suburb

    d. An apartment

45. Who or what is Uachtarán?

    a. A poor person

    b. The president

    c. The minister

    d. A rich person

46. What is the Irish equivalent for the word *plentiful*?

    a. Tops

    b. Galore

    c. Brog

    d. Shanty

answer key

chapter 1
Writers, Musicians, and Actors, Oh, My!

1. a. The Oscar statuette
2. c. Frank McCourt
3. b. 1923
4. d. John McGahern
5. b. The Academy Award–winning screenplay writer of *The Crying Game*
6. c. *Sling Blade*
7. a. Artane Boys' Band
8. c. "Danny Boy"
9. a. Eurovision Song Contest
10. a. Producer and director of *Lord of the Dance*
11. c. U2
12. b. The Irish Film Board
13. c. *I Went Down*
14. a. Kenneth Branagh
15. d. Cong
16. a. Maud Gonne
17. c. Latin
18. d. Doors
19. a. Tara
20. d. Patrick McCabe
21. c. Nick Cave
22. b. Paul Hewson
23. a. Van Morrison
24. c. The Pogues
25. a. Sinéad O'Connor (*Nothing Compares 2 U*)
26. a. Christy Brown
27. d. "Down All the Days"
28. b. Albert Finney
29. a. Pierce Brosnan
30. d. Nuala O'Faolain
31. c. George Bernard Shaw
32. b. Three (William Butler Yeats, George Bernard Shaw, Samuel Beckett)
33. c. *Ulysses*
34. c. Siobhán McKenna
35. b. Frank O'Connor
36. a. The Abbey Theatre
37. c. The O$_2$ (originally the Point Theatre)
38. a. Leon Uris
39. c. *The Informer*
40. d. James Cagney and Pat O'Brien
41. a. Oliver Goldsmith
42. c. *Irish Eyes Are Smiling* (1944), *My Wild Irish Rose* (1947), *Untamed* (1955)
43. a. *I See a Dark Stranger*
44. b. Lady Gregory, Michael McHugh, Frank O'Connor

45. a. *The Plough and the Stars*
46. c. John Huston
47. c. *The Midnight Court*
    (by Brian Merriman)
48. a. Fred Astaire
49. a. The Saw Doctors
50. c. A book by Woody Guthrie
51. b. Rory Gallagher
52. c. Van Morrison
53. c. *The Wall*
54. b. Them
55. d. Paddington, Greater
    London
56. a. William Butler Yeats
57. b. *Playboy of the Western World*
58. c. Oscar Wilde
59. a. Seamus Heaney
60. a. *Finnegans Wake*
61. c. *The Butcher Boy*
62. b. George Russell
63. c. Flute
64. d. Dana
65. d. The Chieftains
66. a. Peadar Kearney
67. b. The selling of children
    as food, to solve Ireland's
    economic problems
68. c. John McCormack
69. d. Midge Ure

chapter 2
**Leprechauns, Banshees,
and Spells**
1. a. To be buried up to the
   neck in moist river sand
2. a. If you move to a new
   house on a Saturday,
   disaster is sure to follow
3. b. The friendship is over

4. d. Sorrow
5. c. Silver
6. a. Powerful wands
7. a. The Rock of Cashel
8. b. You'll die
9. c. There's going to be a
   household argument
10. c. Crowing, whistling, black,
    unlucky
11. b. Tie a bunch of mint
    around one's wrist
12. d. Rheumatism
13. d. A crooked pin
14. a. Someone is speaking
    ill of you
15. b. The snake
16. d. Yellow trefoil
17. a. Lugh
18. c. Tailor and cobbler
19. c. Tory Island
20. d. Sing
21. a. Turn back
22. a. Carrageen moss simmered
    in water and lemon juice
23. d. Cowslip
24. c. Chewing a clove of garlic
25. a. Shrove Tuesday
26. c. Cold and wet
27. a. Whitsunday
28. b. Easter Sunday
29. b. Disaster
30. a. The Danes of old
31. d. A piece of oatmeal cake
32. b. A bottle of whiskey
33. a. Seven
34. c. May Eve, Midsummer
    Eve, November Eve
35. c. Saint John
36. a. The last of the Irish bards

37. b. An ugly creature left by fairies in place of a stolen child
38. c. A relative of the leprechaun
39. b. Banshee
40. b. Fire and iron
41. d. The boar
42. c. Molasses melted in warm water
43. b. Mermaid
44. a. Married a mermaid
45. d. A creature that can transform itself from a seal to a human being
46. b. The Keening
47. b. William Allingham
48. c. A leprechaun on a drinking spree
49. d. A shamrock
50. d. The coming of a storm
51. a. Cúchulainn
52. b. Fionn mac Cumhaill
53. a. Swans
54. d. Nine hundred years
55. c. Beneath mounds of earth
56. b. A black horse with yellow eyes
57. c. The doctrine of the Holy Trinity
58. d. The shamrock
59. b. Lay down their lives for Ireland
60. a. Three
61. c. In the fifth century CE
62. b. It was created by Richard Joyce as a testament of his love for his wife-to-be during his enslavement to a goldsmith
63. d. Both a and b
64. a. It was supposedly cursed by Fionn mac Cumhaill
65. c. The first three days in April
66. a. During the month of May
67. c. Tales of sea journeys
68. d. *Lebor na hUidre, Book of Leinster*, the Rawlinson manuscripts
69. d. The Tuatha Dé Danann
70. a. Brighid

chapter 3
City Folk

1. a. River Liffey
2. b. The postal code for an affluent section of Dublin
3. b. Dublin Area Rapid Transit
4. a. Southeast Dublin
5. b. The Anglo-Normans
6. b. The insignia of the Knights of Saint Patrick
7. c. The rivers of Ireland
8. d. At Trinity College Dublin
9. a. The National Museum of Ireland
10. d. Bank of Ireland
11. a. Leinster House
12. b. Dublin's Lord Mayor
13. a. Arnaldo Pomodoro
14. c. Accept all denominations
15. b. The monks of Iona
16. a. The two chambers of the modern Irish parliament
17. b. Eighteenth century
18. c. A shopping center
19. c. Justice
20. a. Sitric Silkbeard

21. d. Strongbow
22. d. City Assembly House
23. c. Saint Laurence O'Toole
24. b. Tailors' Hall
25. b. In a sacred well next to Saint Patrick's Cathedral
26. a. Fownes Street
27. a. The General Post Office
28. c. Nineteen years
29. d. Both a and b
30. b. Caskets of intact bodies
31. d. O'Connell Street
32. c. The Shelbourne
33. b. Molly Malone
34. c. Tonehenge
35. c. Inside the Shelbourne hotel
36. a. Patrick Pearse
37. d. Joshua Dawson
38. b. The Mansion House
39. c. That every parishioner buy bread for the poor
40. b. The Pale
41. a. Musick Hall
42. b. A person from either the city or county of Dublin
43. a. Savoy and Cineworld
44. c. Donnybrook Rugby Ground
45. c. The Grand and the Royal
46. d. RTE
47. b. The smallest Irish woman ever
48. a. Ten million
49. c. Whitefriar Street Church
50. b. The Martello Tower in Sandycove
51. a. The Ascension
52. c. The Custom House

53. d. The fiftieth anniversary of the 1916 Easter Rising
54. b. A traffic light
55. d. Rope
56. b. It housed the first Jewish temple built in Ireland
57. c. It is Ireland's oldest public library
58. b. A burial ground
59. a. Molly Malone
60. d. The Brazen Head
61. a. The Invincibles
62. c. Robert Emmet
63. b. The 1916 Rising
64. b. June 16
65. d. "Happy the city whose citizens obey"
66. c. Castles
67. b. Charles Stewart Parnell
68. a. Dr. Bartholomew Mosse
69. b. Georgian

chapteR 4
Genuine Grub and Guinness Galore

1. c. Lamb
2. a. Galway
3. c. Porter
4. a. Hot whiskey
5. d. Scones
6. a. Murpheys and Beamish
7. b. Goose
8. b. Salmon
9. c. Varieties of potatoes
10. c. An Irish fast-food chain
11. d. Coddle

12. a. Halloween (colcannon is made from mashed potatoes, cabbage, butter, salt and pepper)
13. c. Trimmings from pork steaks
14. b. A soft-serve cone spiked with a Flake chocolate bar
15. b. Yeast
16. b. A pint of stout
17. d. Both a and b
18. c. Rhyming slang for a gargle (drink)
19. d. A layered mixture of WKD® Blue, Smirnoff® Ice, and Bacardi Breezer® Orange
20. d. Tea
21. a. An awful-tasting cup of tea
22. d. Scallions
23. d. Bacon, egg, sausage, black and white pudding, fried tomato
24. b. Lobster cooked in whiskey and cream
25. c. A site, consisting of a hole in the ground filled with water, for cooking deer
26. b. Irish stew
27. a. Hangovers
28. d. Bacon fat (haggerty is a layered dish of thinly sliced potatoes, onions, and cheese)
29. a. Barley-based whiskey
30. a. Peat
31. c. Potatoes
32. d. Bangers

33. b. A Catholic's betrayal of his religion by converting to Protestantism in order to receive food from the soup kitchens during the 1800s
34. c. Potato chips
35. a. Edible seaweed
36. a. A paramilitary reserve that existed during the Irish War of Independence
37. c. An apple-based soft drink
38. c. Red and white
39. c. Lemonade
40. a. Derry, Northern Ireland
41. d. Loaf and griddle cake
42. a. Drisheen
43. c. Tanora
44. b. A malted bread
45. c. Pan / your man
46. d. Pat Shortt
47. b. 1757
48. c. Joseph Sheridan
49. d. Irish coffee
50. a. Supermarkets
51. c. Brandy butter
52. b. Whiskey
53. a. Two thousand
54. c. "My Goodness, My Guinness"
55. b. Lead
56. a. 1580 / South America
57. b. A fungal disease
58. c. A successful Irish reality television show
59. b. Ballymaloe Cookery School
60. c. Ireland's most famous cook
61. a. Paolo Tullio
62. d. A Zen meditation center

63. c. Chippers
64. b. It is Ireland's oldest fish-and-chip shop
65. a. Irish butter sauce
66. d. Ray
67. a. Kinsale
68. c. A lady's breakfast is served with one egg, while the gentleman's is served with two eggs
69. a. Cheeses

chapter 5
The Fighting Irish
1. a. Swimming
2. b. Hurling
3. b. Thomond Park
4. c. Jaguar
5. c. Gaelic (Athletic Association)
6. c. Croke Park
7. a. Manchester United
8. a. Sean Og O'Hailpin
9. b. Irish National Surfing Champion
10. d. Carne Golf Links
11. c. A hurling ball
12. a. The Curragh
13. b. Win the British Open at Carnoustie
14. d. Jack Nicklaus
15. c. Boxing
16. b. Greyhound racing
17. b. 1967
18. d. The largest thoroughbred racehorse breeding operation
19. d. A family of sports that require navigational skills using a map and a compass
20. c. The All-Ireland Senior Football Championship
21. b. Fifteen
22. a. John M. McAlery
23. c. 1878
24. a. Founding clubs of the Irish Football Association
25. b. Hurling
26. a. The playing of foreign games by its members
27. d. Kevin Cavey
28. c. Sonia O'Sullivan
29. c. 1865
30. b. The position of prime minister
31. a. 1956
32. d. Seán Kelly
33. b. Baseball
34. c. Tennis
35. c. 1884
36. a. Left corner forward

chapter 6
Invasions, Uprisings, and More
1. a. 1775
2. d. Eight
3. b. 1810
4. b. *Shamrock*
5. c. It boasts the longest geographical name in Ireland
6. c. The last witch in Ireland
7. b. Gardening
8. d. A pig
9. b. A single good day of weather
10. a. Dubh Linn

11. a. The Charitable Irish Society of Boston
12. b. Commander of a pirate ship during the 1500s
13. c. Take the longest road home from the church
14. a. A lapel pin
15. c. 1801
16. d. No one
17. a. June 30, 1972
18. c. The Irish Republican Brotherhood
19. a. The Wild Geese
20. a. 1919
21. a. 1955
22. b. Father of the American Navy
23. c. 9000 BCE
24. a. Brian Boru
25. c. Belfast and Dublin
26. c. Six
27. c. Good Friday Agreement
28. b. Brian Boru
29. a. Fifteen
30. a. Derry
31. b. David Trimble
32. b. Henry II
33. a. O'Sullivan
34. b. Wexford
35. b. Tom Barry
36. d. An anti-treaty IRA fighter
37. d. Terence MacSwiney
38. b. 1882
39. a. 500 BCE
40. a. Saint Brendan
41. b. 1922
42. b. Coffin ships
43. c. The United States
44. a. 800 CE
45. a. Daniel O'Connell
46. a. The United States
47. a. Countess Markievicz
48. c. Whiskey
49. b. They were prisoners in Kilmainham Gaol
50 c. Universities for rebels
51. d. A collection of civil laws from the fifth century
52. b. The Vikings
53. d. Tighearnan O'Rourke's
54. d. Hugh de Lacy
55. b. Professional cattle thieves
56. d. Shane O'Neill
57. b. Wolfe Tone
58. a. A pub
59. a. The "travelers," a group of gypsy-like individuals who live on the fringe of society
60. b. A rule that monks wash their hands before and after meals
61. c. He built Blarney Castle
62. d. Cork Harbour Water Club
63. c. She was the first immigrant to pass through Ellis Island
64. a. Mary Francis Cusack
65. c. "Glory to God and peace on earth to men of goodwill."
66. b. The Torc Waterfall in Killarney
67. d. O'Brien

chapter 7

No Time Like the Present

1. d. 4.5 million
2. a. Blue
3. d. Seven years
4. b. 1937
5. b. The Irish prime minister
6. d. Murphy
7. a. Son of
8. a. Irish
9. c. Good Friday and Christmas Day
10. a. Queen Elizabeth I
11. b. The gift of gab
12. b. An annual gathering of traditional Irish musicians and dancers from all around the world
13. c. County Donegal
14. a. Athenry
15. b. Aran
16. c. Phoenix
17. a. Ha'penny Bridge
18. a. The Irish Sea
19. c. Belfast
20. a. The Teflon Taoiseach
21. d. Belfast
22. b. 1997
23. b. They turn in a clockwise direction; the rest of the world's windmills turn counterclockwise
24. a. Brazilian
25. c. Brick throwing between loyalist and nationalist teenagers in mixed Protestant and Catholic areas
26. b. Software
27. d. Between 40 million and 44 million
28. a. January 6
29. b. The traditional day for Irish women to ignore their housework
30. a. Fort of the Harlot
31. b. The Celtic harp
32. a. 302 miles
33. b. Third biggest
34. a. Ériu
35. c. Huey Morgan of Fun Lovin' Criminals
36. d. Guinness Storehouse
37. a. Dublin's best-known department store
38. d. Kerry
39. d. NATO
40. d. Four
41. a. William Butler Yeats
42. a. 353
43. b. The Celtic harp
44. c. Polish
45. c. Saint Bridget
46. a. The Spire of Dublin
47. c. Three
48. b. Aer Lingus
49. c. London to Dublin
50. a. Allied Irish Banks, Bank of Ireland, National Irish Bank, Ulster Bank
51. c. A charitable organization that sends refurbished computers from Ireland to educational institutions in sub-Saharan Africa
52. d. The 50th anniversary of the Treaty of Rome

53. a. The 100th anniversary of Samuel Beckett's birth
54. b. Flax fibers
55. d. Wind
56. a. Twenty-four
57. b. A café
58. c. Harry Clarke
59. c. Term used to describe the period of rapid economic growth in the 1990s
60. a. An elongated whale-shaped hill formed by glacial action
61. b. They are all names of lighthouses
62. c. Killarney and Belfast
63. b. There is no national park in Northern Ireland
64. c. An artificial island, used as a settlement

chapter 8
Hopes, Dreams, and Fulfillment
1. c. New York
2. d. Charles Thomson
3. d. 130,000
4. c. 25 percent
5. b. 25,000
6. d. All of the above
7. c. 1737
8. c. Missouri
9. c. 1936
10. b. Jack Dempsey
11. a. Anthony Quinn
12. b. James Hoban
13. d. Nine
14. c. City Hall
15. c. Hugh O'Brien
16. a. No Irish Need Apply

17. a. Middlesex
18. a. Murphies
19. c. 50 percent
20. a. Al Smith
21. b. Delaware, Massachusetts, New Hampshire
22. d. Twenty-three
23. b. Savannah
24. d. Andrew Jackson
25. d. All of the above
26. b. County Offaly
27. c. Chicago, Boston, Jersey City
28. b. 1843
29. a. Someone of Irish heritage who was not born in Ireland
30. c. William Bonney
31. a. "Biddys"
32. a. Workingmen's Benevolent Association
33. d. John Alcock and Arthur Brown
34. a. Annie Glover
35. d. Philadelphia
36. c. Alexander Turney Stewart
37. c. Patrick Ford
38. a. Jeremiah O'Brien
39. d. James J. Braddock
40. b. Mother Jones
41. c. Father Edward J. Flanagan
42. b. *Moby Dick*
43. b. Ballyporeen
44. c. 1963
45. b. A wreath
46. d. One penny
47. d. All of the above
48. b. Twenty-five

49. c. The Winter Hill Gang
50. a. Blue

chapteR 9
Who Said What?

1. c. Brendan Behan
2. b. James Joyce
3. b. Jonathan Swift
4. a. George Best
5. d. Winston Churchill
6. b. Michael Collins
7. c. Edna O'Brien
8. b. George Bernard Shaw
9. d. "Thanks"
10. b. He sent a reply that read, "Mr. George Bernard Shaw likewise"
11. c. Neighs
12. a. John Berryman
13. c. Seamus Heaney
14. a. Ian Paisley
15. b. Reproduce
16. d. John Hume
17. a. Sean Kelly
18. c. Maria Edgeworth
19. c. Eddie Hackett
20. a. The Ring of Kerry golf course
21. c. George Washington
22. a. "My Wild Irish Mother"
23. b. His cleaning lady
24. b. Pope John Paul II
25. c. James Buchanan
26. b. Marianne Moore
27. b. Jimmy Walker
28. d. Bram Stoker
29. b. Gold and diamonds, who owe their value only to their scarcity
30. c. Virginia Woolf
31. b. toads, adders, noisome
32. c. "I, the poet William Yeats / With old millboards and sea-green slates…"
33. c. Mary, the Rose of Tralee
34. c. Chicago mayor Richard Daley
35. a. Oscar Wilde
36. d. No taste
37. a. Bono
38. b. *My Left Foot*
39. a. James Joyce
40. c. George Bernard Shaw
41. b. "Because the price of a pint of orange juice is twice the price of a pint of stout."
42. a. "Leave it on."
43. d. "Thank you, Sister, and may you be the mother of a bishop."
44. c. He returned the tickets with a note saying, "Could I have tickets for the second night—if there is one?"
45. d. *Drums Under the Window*
46. a. Sean O'Casey
47. d. William Butler Yeats
48. a. May they never meet!
49. d. Colin Farrell
50. a. Being a woman: "Everyone says you're important and nice, but you take second place all the time."

chapter 10
But What Does It Mean?

1. b. The events of 1607, when the Earl of Tyrone went into exile, taking other lords with him
2. c. "Are youse all right in the back there, lads?"
3. a. Whiskey
4. b. Things that are traditional and usually pretty rough
5. b. "Middling"
6. b. A storyteller
7. a. A few drinks
8. a. A haircut
9. c. "Scaldy"
10. b. Cut a hole in the door, stuck his arm through, and invited his rival to shake hands
11. c. Heavy boots
12. b. A cloak
13. b. To commit suicide in the Shannon River
14. a. The police
15. d. Father Matthew Theobald
16. c. The whiskey that evaporates from the barrels during the maturation period of five to twelve years (also the name of a bar in New York City)
17. c. A Baby Guinness mixes Bailey's and Guinness; a Johnny Jump Up mixes Guinness and cider
18. a. Poteen
19. b. The Houlihans
20. c. Behave yourself
21. b. "Ireland forever"
22. a. Have fun
23. c. Going grocery shopping
24. c. Two black eyes
25. a. Good fortune
26. b. Tomorrow
27. c. Moustache
28. a. Ronald Colman
29. a. Drunk
30. a. A person who runs a saloon or inn
31. c. Megaceros
32. c. A cairn
33. d. Both a and b
34. a. Cennedi
35. b. The Irish tradition of an evening spent with story-telling by the fire
36. a. I'm *quern* tired.
37. c. Muscles
38. b. The Americans
39. d. A small house or cabin
40. c. Ecker
41. a. "Milly up!"
42. c. A wig
43. d. Both a and b
44. b. A rough area
45. b. The president
46. a. Tops